DICTIONARY OF HYPNOSIS

DICTIONARY
OF
HYPNOSIS

by

RALPH B. WINN, Ph. D.

Adjunct Professor of Psychology

Rollins College

PHILOSOPHICAL LIBRARY

New York

Printed in the United States of America

A

ABREACTION, see: *"Catharsis."*

ABULIA: Loss or impairment of will power.

ADLER, ALFRED (1870-1937): Austrian psychiatrist, originally a follower of S. Freud, and the founder of the movement known as Individual Psychology. His last years were spent in the U. S. A.

AGE REGRESSION: The phenomenon of returning in one's mind as well as in one's behavior to some earlier stage of life, with amnesia of the entire subsequent period. This can occur spontaneously, for instance in senile people; or it can be induced by hypnosis almost at any age.

Hypnotic age regression is disorientation "with relation to person, place or time" (M. V. Kline, in the *Journal of Clinical and Experimental Hypnosis,* 1953).

ALCOHOLISM: Addiction to alcoholic beverages. Hypnotism and suggestion have been used to control or overcome it.

If he discovers that "alcohol relieves his tension, the patient is likely to become an alcoholic" (S. J. Van Pelt in the *Medical Hypnosis Handbook*).

"Comparison of data obtained in three different types of treatment of alcoholism shows that the most desirable affect is reached by means of hypnotherapy, by itself or in combination with apomorphine. . . .

"The therapeutic effect, in cases of alcoholism, is increased in proportion to the depth of the hypnotic state attained, from which follows the advantage of inducing, whenever possible, the somnambulistic state. . . .

"It is recommended that an average course of hypnotic treatment consist of nine to twelve sessions. In alcoholism of long duration, it may be necessary to extend the number of sessions up to fifteen" (T. N. Gordova and N. K. Kovalev, in the *Psychotherapy in the Soviet Union*).

"An interesting and important motion picture 'Once and Forever' was produced a few years ago; it dealt with the treatment of alcoholics by hypnosis. There were three parts to it. The first part had to do with alcoholism as a social evil affecting the family, everyday life and industry. The content was not merely educational; it also served as a warning or emotional preparation. The second part of the film portrayed a hypnotic session with a medical purpose. The public saw a group of individuals on the screen, all suffering from alcoholism in various stages and forms; they also had an opportunity to see Professor Y. V. Kannabih putting the patients to sleep. The third part constituted an attempt to hypnotize the living audience. It aimed at mass hypnosis conducted directly from the screen. All the stages of therapeutic influence were organically brought together thus increasing the influence of suggestion. Examination of the results showed the high psychotherapeutic effectiveness of the picture.

"Unfortunately, the number of films of this caliber is comparatively small" (L. M. Sukharebsky, in the *Psychotherapy in the Soviet Union*).

ALIENIST: Specialist in psychiatry from the standpoint of law.

ALLERGY: Excessive sensitivity to a substance.

AMNESIA: Loss of ability to recall past experiences. It may cover a large field of memories or be confined to specific episodes. Suggestion or hypnosis is often helpful in removing it temporarily and occasionally permanently. It can also be induced by hypnosis or arise spontaneously with regard to occurrences in the state of trance.

"Amnesia will be resorted to where repression of a memory serves an important defensive purpose" (L. R. Wolberg, *Hypnoanalysis*).

"Experimental evidence indicates that 'amnesic' hypnotic subjects *recognize* the material which they claim that they do not remember" (T. X. Barber, in the *Archives of General Psychiatry*, 1962).

"Hypnosis merely removes the block or inhibition in the case of hysterical or traumatic amnesias" (C. L. Hull, *Hypnosis and Suggestibility*).

3

AMNESIA, AUTOHYPNOTIC: Self-induced repression of certain memories. It occurs as a simple defense mechanism.

AMNESIA, LOCALIZED: Loss of memory with regard to an incident, experience, place, or time.

AMNESIA, POST-HYPNOTIC: Loss of memory for happenings occurring during hypnosis or, selectively, for whatever the hypnotist suggested to forget.

"Most hypnotists seem to encourage and actually to suggest amnesia subsequent to the sitting. But in most cases this is quite superfluous. . . . With Schilder and Kauders, I contend that 'we do not consider it an advantage to have the patient kept in ignorance of what is happening to him. . . . I do not know of any advantage in producing amnesia in *every* case" (*Scientific Hypnotism*).

AMNESIA, SPONTANEOUS: A form of amnesia occurring in a subject without receiving any suggestion to this effect.

"Spontaneous amnesia . . . is a simple psychological defense mechanism" (Ainslie Meares, "The Atavistic Theory of Hypnosis," *Transactions of the* 1961 *International Congress on Hypnosis*).

ANALGESIA: Local or widespread loss of the sense of pain. It can be induced by suggestion or hypnosis.

"Sometimes this exists to such a degree that the severest surgical operations can be performed during the state. It is also known that needles may be run into some persons during hypnosis without their feeling pain" (A. Moll, *Hypnosis*).

4

ANALYTICAL PSYCHOLOGY: A variety of psycho-analysis developed by C. G. Jung (1875-1946), a leading Swiss psychiatrist, postulating the existence of the collective unconscious and employing the technique of mental analysis and synthesis.

ANAMNESIS: A systematic account of a subject's experiences and state of health prior to treatment. It is to be distinguished from catamnesis which is the follow-up record subsequent to treatment.

ANESTHESIA: Insensibility, loss of sensitivity. It may be caused by organic or psychological conditions and confined to a large or small region. In the field of hypnotic experimentation, the term refers to the temporary loss of sensory experience, that is, of sight, hearing, taste, etc. The use of hypnosis in surgery makes it possible to perform painless operations, whenever the use of ordinary anaesthetics is counter-indicated.

ANIMAL HYPNOSIS: Hypnosis insofar as it is applicable to animals.
"I am inclined to think that in many instances it is a conscious simulation of death, adopted by the animals from the instinctive knowledge of the fact that certain birds and beasts of prey . . . will not attack what is dead" (J. M. Bramwell, *Hypnotism*).

ANIMAL MAGNETISM: Mesmer's name for hypnotism selected on the assumption that the state is related to the phenomenon of ordinary magnetism.
"1. A responsive influence exists between the heavenly bodies, the earth, and animated bodies.

5

"2. A fluid universally diffused, so continuous as not to admit of a vacuum, incomparably subtle, and naturally susceptible of receiving, propagating, and communicating all motor disturbances, is the means of this influence. . . .

"4. Alternative effects result from this action, which may be considered to be a flux and reflux. . . .

"8. The animal body experiences the alternative effects of this agent, and is directly affected by its insinuation into the substance of the nerves.

"9. Properties are displayed, analogous to those of the magnet, particularly in the human body, in which diverse and opposite poles are likewise to be distinguished, and these may be communicated, changed, destroyed, and reinforced. . . .

"10. This property of the human body which renders it susceptible of the influence of the heavenly bodies, and of the reciprocal action of those which environ it, manifests its analogy with the magnet, and this has decided me to adopt the term of animal magnetism.

"11. The action and virtue of animal magnetism, thus characterized, may be communicated to other animate or inanimate bodies. Both these classes of bodies, however, vary in their susceptibility. . . .

"17. This magnetic virtue may be accumulated, concentrated, and transported. . . .

"20. The magnet, whether natural or artificial, is like other bodies susceptible of animal magnetism, and even of the opposite virtue: in neither case does its action on fire and on the needle suffer any change, and this shows that the principle of animal magnetism essentially differs from that of mineral magnetism.

"21. This system sheds new light upon the nature of fire

and of light, as well as on the theory of attraction, of flux and reflux, of the magnet and of electricity.

"22. It teaches us that the magnet and artificial electricity have, with respect to diseases, properties common to a host of other agents presented to us by nature, and that if the use of these has been attended by some useful results, they are due to animal magnetism.

"23. These facts show, in accordance with the practical rules I am about to establish, that this principle will cure nervous diseases directly, and other diseases indirectly.

"24. By its aid the physician is enlightened as to the use of medicine, and may render its action more perfect, and he can provoke and direct salutary crises, so as completely to control them.

"25. In communicating my method, I shall, by a new theory of matter, demonstrate the universal utility of the principle I seek to establish.

"26. Possessed of this knowledge, the physician may judge with certainty of the origin, nature, and progress of diseases, however complicated they may be; he may hinder their development and accomplish their cure without exposing the patient to dangerous and troublesome consequences, irrespective of age, temperament, and sex. Even women in a state of pregnancy, and during parturition, may reap the same advantage.

"27. This doctrine will finally enable the physician to decide upon the health of every individual, and of the presence of the diseases to which he may be exposed. In this way the art of healing may be brought to absolute perfection" (F. A. Mesmer's propositions as given in the English translation of A. Binet and Ch. Féré's *Animal Magnetism*).

ANXIETY: An emotional and sometimes recurring attitude related to fear or worry. It may arise in connection with unfamiliar, exciting, painful, or dangerous situations. It commonly leads to tension, depression, irritability and, somewhat indirectly, to headaches, gastro-intestinal as well as sexual disturbances — most of which can be relieved by medical hypnosis.

APHASIA, FUNCTIONAL: Loss of power of speech as a result of psychological causes, usually regarded as a symptom of hysteria. It can be successfully overcome by hypnotic treatment.

ASSOCIATION OF IDEAS: This term suggested by John Locke (1632-1704) refers to the connection of ideas in the stream of human consciousness.

ASSOCIATIVE LEARNING: The type of learning emphasizing the natural connection of ideas or images among themselves.

ASTHMA, BRONCHIAL: A chronic disorder of breathing of emotional or allergic origin. The former type can be successfully treated by hypnosis.

"The patients suffering from bronchial asthma manifest, under the influence of hypnosis, positive changes in many organic functions: breathing improves, the lung capacity increases, the arterial pressure rises. Treatment by hypnosis has been statistically justified. Forty-two patients (out of 100) showed much improvement and had no attacks for the duration of six months to three years. Twenty-eight patients were well improved; the attacks were conspicuously milder and rarer. The rest showed no significant change" (I. I. Bull, in *Psychotherapy in the Soviet Union*).

ATAVISTIC THEORY OF HYPNOSIS: According to Ainslie Meares' views, suggestion in general is a primitive function long preceding the appearance of logical thought. And hypnosis, insofar as it results in complete acceptance of the hypnotic authority, is a kind of regression expressed in the loss of critical inclinations or ability.

ATTENTION: Focusing one's consciousness on something that appears important, interesting or startling and the corresponding adjustment of one's sensory apparatus so as to facilitate optimal activity in this connection. Attention may be aroused from outside (involuntary) or from inside (voluntary).

AUTO-HYPNOSIS: Auto-hypnosis is a kind of verbal conditioning as developed by Andrew Salter and explained in his *What Is Hypnosis?* In this procedure, a person developed into a good subject and thoroughly trained in proper instructions is allowed to carry on by himself. In other words, the trance is subsequently induced by the 'subject' himself and he alone retains control of what is to follow. As Dr. Salter puts it himself, "Suggestions . . . may come from within or without. As long as you cooperate, with me or with yourself, the suggestions work."

AUTOMATIC DRAWING: Drawing on paper (or doodling) without being aware of doing this.

AUTOMATIC WRITING: Writing words or even whole sentences without being aware of it.

9

"The hypnotized patient was at the time engaged in automatic writing and, as I talked, he started writing about his resentment toward an elder sister with whom he had fought as a child. In the process he recalled an early experience that had a traumatic effect on him" (L. R. Wolberg, *Hypnoanalysis*).

"Automatic writing can be employed with many patients to help them write out conflicts, fears, anxieties" (M. H. Erickson, S. Hershman, I. I. Secter, *The Practical Application of Medical and Dental Hypnosis*).

AUTOMATISM: Human activity that is carried out without any conscious awareness of it. This includes some simple forms of behavior (i. e., tics) as well as highly complex actions ranging from automatic writing or drawing to sleepwalking.

AUTONOMIC NERVOUS SYSTEM: It is a vast involuntary system of widely distributed nerve fibers which innervate smooth muscles and glands. It is divided into the sympathetic and parasympathetic sub-systems. The viscera are generally innervated by both, though in the opposite manner. The A. N. S. plays a vital role in respiration, digestion, circulation of blood, and the activity of glands of internal and external secretion.

"Increased control over the autonomic nervous system, so common in hypnosis, is responsible for many striking psychosomatic phenomena" (S. J. Van Pelt, in *Medical Hypnosis Handbook*).

"This system is primarily reflexive, controlling and regulating bodily functions which require no cooperation of consciousness or intellect; yet it is not fully involuntary as it is continually, almost constantly influenced by two related types

10

of experience, namely by emotion and by suggestion" (*Scientific Hypnotism*).

AUTO-SUGGESTION: Suggestion made to oneself. It may be a product of wishful thinking or, more rationally, of self-persuasion. It is best exemplified by the famous recipe publicly offered by Emile Coué: "Every day in every way I am getting better and better." And as long as people remembered him, it worked.

"Once we comprehend the nature of the mechanism of suggestion, it is not difficult to infer that what is known as auto-suggestion can be used apart from somebody inspiring the subject only in exceptional cases" (*Scientific Hypnotism*).

AWARENESS: Conscious apprehension of an event, situation, bodily condition, feeling, or mental experience.

B

BAQUET: Mesmer's (1733-1815) device for mass hypnosis and treatment of his patients. It was a kind of large oaken tub, about two feet high, filled with water, iron filings, bottles, and ground glass, around which about thirty persons could be standing and touching iron rods protruding from the tub. A contact with them was supposed to originate magnetic currents. In combination with animal magnetism (hypnotic suggestion) the baquet presumably had healing power.

BEKHTEREV, VLADIMIR M. (1857-1927): A student of Charcot (1825-1893) and eventually a famous Russian psychiatrist, reflexologist and founder of the Psychoneurological Institute in St. Petersburg (now Leningrad), in which considerable research work in hypnosis was going on.

13

BERNHEIM, HIPPOLYTE M. (1840-1919): A French psychotherapist and the leading member of the Nancy School, who studied and experimented with phenomena of hypnotism. His *Suggestive Therapeutics* (1886) is generally regarded as the first scientific book in the field.

BINET, ALFRED (1857-1911): A French psychologist and educator, the creator of early intelligence tests for children (with Th. Simon) as well as the author (with C. Féré) of *Animal Magnetism* (1888).

BIO-MAGNETISM, see: *"Animal Magnetism."*

BLUSHING: Involuntary vasodilation, particularly in the face. This is a phenomenon of psychological origin, which can be occasionally embarrassing. It can be usually cured by a few hypnotic sessions.

BRAID, JAMES (1795-1860): A Manchester, England, physician and the author of *Neurypnology* (1843) who discovered that the so-called "animal magnetism" had actually nothing to do with any magnetic influences and consequently gave the modern name to the science of hypnotism. He used at first the method of fascination, but later turned to verbal suggestion. Among other things, he availed himself of hypnosis to perform painless surgical operations.

"The hypnotic state is essentially a state of mental concentration in which the faculties of the mind of the patient are so engrossed with a single idea or train of thought as, for the nonce, to be dead or indifferent to all other considerations and influences" (*Neurypnology*).

"My researches prove the power of concentration of at-

14

tention, as not only capable of changing physical action, so as to make some patients, in the wide-waking state, imagine that they see and feel from an external influence what is due entirely to an internal or mental cause; but I have extended the researches, so as to prove that the same law obtains in respect to all the other organs of special sense, and different functions of the body. My theoretical views, therefore, instead of diminishing, rather enhance the value of this power as a means of cure. They strikingly prove how much may be achieved by proper attention to, and direction of, this power of the human mind over the physical frame, and vice versa, in ameliorating the ills which flesh is heir to" (J. Braid, "The Power of the Mind over the Body," a pamphlet, J. Churchill, London, 1846).

BRAIDISM: The theory of hypnosis offered by James Braid, a British physician and surgeon. According to him, hypnosis has nothing to do with "magnetic" forces of nature; rather, it represents bodily consequences of suggestion under conditions of trance. Such a state, he decided, opens many new opportunities for curing bodily ailments.

BRUXISM: The gnashing of teeth, usually during sleep and consequently unconsciously. Insofar as the habit is psychological in origin, it can be treated by means of hypnosis, provided its basic cause is properly identified.

C

CAPTIVATION: M. Hirsch's name for the state of light hypnosis.

CASE HISTORY: The technique for studying individual cases by recording relevant circumstances of their life.

CASE STUDY: Study of individual subjects by the clinical method.

CATALEPSY: A form of high suggestibility in which the subject manifests rigidity of the limbs and can be 'molded' by putting him in various postures. It is occasionally found in mental and brain diseases, such as hysteria or schizophrenia, and can be suggested in the state of hypnosis.

"The patients make no movements of their own volition; but, if they are placed in no matter how uncomfortable attitude, they maintain it for a very long time" (E. Bleuler, *Textbook of Psychiatry*).

"Catalepsy is never observed in the writer's laboratory unless specific suggestion is given" (C. L. Hull, *Hypnosis and Suggestibility*).

"I often use catalepsy of the eyelids with children, as a method of inducing hypnosis. I tell the child to close his eyes so tightly that by the time I count ten he will not be able to open them, and that the more he tries to open them the more they will be stuck together. With cooperative children catalepsy works extremely well" (A. P. Magonet, *The Healing Voice*).

CATAMNESIS: The case history of a subject or patient, particularly in the 'follow-up' period.

CATHARSIS: The technique of working off pent-up emotions, particularly those which disturb or worry the subject; this is done through the process of sharing or acting them out, thus achieving considerable relief. The method of 'free association' or that of hypnotic suggestion can be used to bring 'traumatic' experiences into consciousness.

"Emotional purging by talking out or acting out repressed or partially repressed harmful material" (B. S. Frohman, *Brief Psychotherapy*).

CHARCOT, JEAN-MARTIN (1825-1893): A French psychiatrist and professor of pathology, whose work at the Salpêtrière hospital in Paris was practically confined to hysterical subjects, mainly female, on the assumption that hysteria and hypnotic phenomena are basically related.

His method was "sudden, startling, shocking" (S. L. Krebs, *The Fundamental Principles of Hypnosis*) exemplified by "the sudden sound of a Chinese gong or a bright light suddenly thrown into the eyes."

CHEVREUL-PENDULUM: A portable contraption, originally designed by M. Chevreul, involving a pendulum (a weight suspended by a string about 15 inches long) swaying over a white carton chart on which two lines are drawn crossing at right angles. It is sometimes used to determine and increase the subject's suggestibility or one's own power of concentration.

CHILDBIRTH: "The pains of childbirth are of two kinds; natural and suggested. The suggested pains develop as a result of widespread conviction that they are inevitable. This conviction has been cultivated from generation to generation and affirmed and reaffirmed by relatives and friends, and also by religious circles, medicine and literature. . . .

"We are able to report on the results of suggested painless birth in one thousand cases. Seven hundred of them had prophylactic preparation while three hundred underwent suggestion of painlessness only during the process of childbirth. In eighty percent of all cases there was marked positive effect, and in forty percent there was no pain whatsoever. . . .

"Suggestive preparation should preferably begin early during consultations. This can be followed by suggestions of painless birth. During these sessions all negative emotions connected with pregnancy and childbirth should be removed and replaced by positive emotions. . . .

"These suggestions can be conducted individually or collectively. For the latter purpose groups of thirty or thirty-five women are indicated. The cases of first pregnancy react on the whole better to suggestion than others.

"Suggestion works particularly well in the presence of psychotherapist at the time of childbirth. He may prefer the woman to be in a waking state, so that she could know what happens and to cooperate with the processes of birth. But it cannot be denied that the best results are still obtained in deep hypnotic sleep" (V. I. Zdravomyslov, in the *Psychotherapy in the Soviet Union*).

"Studies conducted by M. Y. Miloslavsky . . . show that, in cases of impending miscarriage, suggestions during hypnotic sleep have been able to reduce excitability of the uterus, to quiet down painful cramps, and to terminate bloody discharges. Of 387 such cases, eighty-seven percent resulted in normal birth" (K. I. Platonov, *ibid.*).

CHILDREN'S SUGGESTIBILITY: It is a well known observation that children are more suggestible than adults. According to the investigations by R. Messerschmidt, this is statistically true of children between the ages of 5 and 14.

CLINICAL DEMONSTRATION: Presentation of one or more cases, with proper explanation, to a number of professional people or students.

COMPLEX: A combination of emotionally charged mental elements. Many psychoanalysts regard complexes as repressed and consequently unconscious.

COMPULSION: An irresistible impulse and the resulting action, sometimes done contrary to the person's conscious will and good sense.

CONCENTRATION: Continuous effort to keep one's attention on an object, topic or work.

CONDITION, TO: To establish a learned, or 'conditioned' emotion, response or reflex.

CONDITIONED EMOTION: An emotion established by, and linked to, particular stimuli, situations or experiences.

CONDITIONED REFLEX: A seemingly simple and easy neural response to something, acquired by way of a stimulus or a combination of stimuli. The term was originated by I. P. Pavlov (1849-1936), a Russian physiologist and psychologist.
"We can regard each case of effective suggestion as the simplest form of conditioned reflex" (I. P. Pavlov, *Conditioned Reflexes*).

CONDITIONED RESPONSE: A habitual response to something, complex or simple, which has been established by a stimulus connecting the two.

CONSCIENCE: Personal judgment of right and wrong. The 'inner' voice. It is usually influenced by public and family opinion.
"Our conscience is a form of fear" (Gregory Zilboorg, *Mind, Medicine and Man*).

CONSCIOUSNESS: The characteristic of all awareness by virtue of which everything is experienced by a person from a point of view and as an item in the chronological continuity of his mental life. The opposite of unconsciousness.
"The greater part of what we call conscious knowledge

21

must in any case exist for very considerable periods of time in a condition of latency" (S. Freud, *Collected Papers, IV*).

"An abstraction like 'the mental is the conscious' is a prejudice" (S. Freud, *Delusion and Dream*).

"We cannot speak of loss of consciousness in hypnosis; and the opinion held by many that a hypnotized subject is generally unconscious is a mistake" (A. Moll, *The Study of Hypnosis*).

CONSENT (for hypnosis): The subject to be hypnotized is sometimes advised that his consent should be put in writing, but if the relationship between the patient and the hypnotist is as it should be there will be good faith on both sides, and no call for such a formality. In the case of minors it is essential that a responsible adult, the parent or guardian, should consent.

CONTENTION: Concentration on some task, interpreted negatively, that is, emphasizing the importance of *not* removing one's attention to something else.

"Contention is a psychological equivalent of attention, minus effort. . . . It simultaneously presupposes the habit of attention and that of relaxation" (Charles Baudouin, *Suggestion and Autosuggestion*).

"If hypnosis increases suggestibility, this may be dependent on various features of hypnosis . . . but for the most part it is due to contention, which annuls voluntary effort, a condition unfavorable to suggestion, while maintaining attention, a condition above all others indispensable to suggestion" (*Ibid.*).

COUÉ, EMILE (1857-1926): A member of the Nancy School of hypnotism and the originator of the technique of waking auto-suggestion made widely known through the formula of "Every day in every way I am getting better and better." He made a very successful lecture tour in the U. S. A. in 1923.

COUNTER-SUGGESTION: A suggestion offered to an individual to challenge his fixed ideas concerning something or to inhibit the effect of a previous belief.

D

DANGERS OF HYPNOSIS: Every amateur should know that insufficient knowledge of, and skill in, hypnotizing presents certain dangers to himself as well as to his subjects. In dealing with human beings, whether young or old, he should know that fear of the unknown or unusual may lead people to misunderstanding, excessive expectations and resulting disappointments as well as to worry, perhaps even alarm. As a result, there is always a chance of legal implications and complications, the more so that subjects (and their parents or relatives, as the case may be) are afflicted with neuroses as often as any other people and may exaggerate their troubles, real or imaginary. Consequently, every measure of precaution and safety, including signed permission to hypnotize, should

25

be taken. Fortunately for all concerned, however, the history of hypnosis demonstrates that it is surprisingly safe, everything considered, especially for the professional specialists in the field.

"There is a danger which it is important to recognize and which I am going to mention. After having been hypnotized a certain number of times, some subjects preserve a disposition to go to sleep spontaneously. Some have been hardly awakened when they fall to sleep again of themselves in the same hypnotic sleep. Others fall asleep thus during the day. This tendency to auto-hypnotization may be repressed by suggestion. It is sufficient to state to the subject during sleep that when once awakened, he will be completely awake, and will not be able to go to sleep again spontaneously during the day" (H. M. Bernheim, *Suggestive Therapeutics*).

"Must we proscribe a thing which may be efficacious, because the occasional abuse of it is injurious? No one proscribes wine, alcohol, opium, quinine, because the immoderate or intemperate use of these substances may bring about accidents. Doubtless suggestion used by dishonest or awkward men is a dangerous practice. Law can and should intervene to repress its abuse" (*Ibid.*)

"The literature offers little credible information concerning possible detrimental effects of experimental hypnosis, although replete with dogmatic and opinionated denunciations founded on outworn and untenable concepts of the phenomenon. The author's own experience, based upon several thousand trances on approximately three hundred individual subjects, some of whom were hypnotized at least five hundred times each over a period of four to six years, reveals no evidence of such harmful effects" (M. H. Erickson, in the *Journal of Abnormal and Social Psychology*, 1932).

"The harm resulting from hypnotism is infinitesimal compared with the good it has accomplished. In fact, no art ever practised has so little evil to be responsible for, either through intent or accident" (W. W. Cook, *Practical Lessons in Hypnotism*).

"A subject of good moral character . . . will not accept a suggestion under hypnosis that is in conflict with his moral convictions or settled principles" (S. L. Krebs, *The Fundamental Principles of Hypnosis*).

"While some people cannot be made to carry out hypnotic suggestions contrary to their principles, there are certainly *some* who can" (S. Edmunds, *Hypnotism and the Supernormal*).

DEATH: A number of learned men, among them O. G. Wetterstrand and A. Munthe, reported that no remedy exerts so soothing an influence on the dying person as hypnotic suggestion.

"Even more striking is the beneficial effect of this method in the most painful of all operations, as a rule still to be endured without anaesthesia — Death. What it was granted to me to do for many of our dying soldiers during the last war is enough to make me thank God for having had this powerful weapon in my hands. In the autumn of 1915 I spent two unforgettable days and nights among a couple of hundred dying soldiers, huddled together under their bloodstained great-coats on the floor of a village church in France. We had no morphia, no chloroform, no anaesthetics whatever to alleviate their tortures and shorten their agony. Many of them died before my eyes, insensible and unaware, often even a smile on their lips, with my hand on their forehead, my slowly repeated words of hope and comfort resounding in their ears, the terror of death gradually vanishing from their closing eyes" (A. Munthe, *The Story of San Michele*).

DEEP HYPNOSIS, see: *"Somnambulism, II."*

DEFENSE MECHANISM: A pattern of self-protective behavior. It may have "the function of keeping from consciousness undesirable or painful thoughts" (Ernest Jones, *Papers on Psycho-Analysis*) and other unhappy experiences.

DEHYPNOTIZATION: Termination of a hypnotic state in an individual or a group.
"It is nearly always possible to put an end to the hypnosis by mental means, that is, by the command to wake up, or to wake up at a particular signal" (A. Moll, *Hypnotism*).
"Sometimes it is extremely difficult to bring a patient back to the waking state for the reason that the hypnotic sleep has become transformed, quite independently of the hypnotist, into a hysterical sleep" (P. Janet, *Psychological Healing*).

DEHYPNOTIZE, TO: To bring somebody out of the hypnotic state. This is usually done by the hypnotist himself, though it is quite possible in advance to transfer the responsibility to another person.

DELUSION: A false belief formed through a mental disease, emotional influence, or ignorance of actual facts.

DENTAL HYPNOSIS: Hypnosis used in dentistry, mainly to minimize pain.
"I witnessed an operation in a dental surgeon's office. The dentist was cutting deeply into the patient's gum. The patient sat back, composed and comfortable, though no drug had

been administered. She had merely been hypnotized. The hypnotist had told her to relax. He had said that she would feel no pain.

"At the conclusion of the operation, which lasted about half an hour, the dentist laid his instruments aside, and nodded to the hypnotist. The latter then addressed the patient: 'When I wake you, there will be no pain, no headache, no after-effects. You'll feel well and happy. Now when I count to ten you'll wake up.'

"Upon the final count, she opened her eyes and smiled. 'When does he begin?' she asked" (R. H. Rhodes, *Hypnosis: Theory, Practice and Application*).

"Most dental operations can be performed under deep hypnosis without pain or discomfort, with the minimum loss of blood and shock" (G. Ambrose and G. Newbold, *A Handbook of Medical Hypnosis*).

DEPERSONALIZATION: The loss of self-identity or self-reality. The subject may be indeed induced by means of hypnosis to forget his name, address, even his past and thus to become temporarily a person without identity.

DERMATOSIS: Skin disease. According to studies conducted by I. A. Zhukov in Sochi and Matsesta, well-known Caucasian resorts (*Psychotherapy in the Soviet Union*), hypnotic treatment of dermatoses brings about excellent results, especially when it is combined with traditional methods of treatment. Out of 135 cases of eczema, for instance, 45 recovered completely and only 2 showed no improvement at all; out of 80 cases of neuro-dermatitis 30 recovered and only 3 showed no improvement; and out of 72 cases of psoriasis 14 were cured and the rest improved. A follow-up study "overwhelmingly testified to the permanent nature of the improvements."

DISCRIMINATION: Perception of difference between two or more similar qualities or things. Discrimination can be improved by hypnosis.

DISSOCIATION: Temporary or lasting separation or even isolation of mental areas exemplified by sleep walking, automatic writing, a double or multiple personality, and other abnormal phenomena, most of which can be demonstrated in normal people under hypnosis.
"Is it suggestion or dissociation which is really the fundamental cause of hypnosis?" (G. H. Estabrooks, *Hypnotism*).

DISTRACTION: Withdrawal of attention from something or attention reacting to different stimuli.

DONATISM: A form of hypnosis emphasizing imitation. It was developed by Alfred d'Hont (1845-1900) whose professional name was Donato.

DREAM: A conscious, story-like episode experienced during sleep. According to S. Freud (1856-1939) and his followers, dreams play a significant symbolic role, the correct interpretation of which may be of considerable value in the psychoanalytic treatment of each patient.
"The strongest minds cannot escape from the hallucinatory suggestions of their dreams" (H. Bernheim, *Suggestive Therapeutics*).
"I believe . . . that we all dream continuously when we are asleep" (A. Forel, *Hypnotism*).

"The dream is the fulfillment of a wish" (S. Freud, *The Interpretation of Dreams*).

"The dream is the guardian of sleep, not the disturber of it" (*Ibid.*).

DREAM, HYPNOTIC: A dream suggested by the hypnotist, whatever be the purpose.

"Verbal stimuli serve as effective instigation of hypnotic dreams. . . . Direct examination of the hypnotic dreams fails to reveal any additional characteristic that would serve to differentiate them from non-hypnotic dreams" (D. B. Klein, in the *University of Texas Bulletin* No. 3009, 1930).

DREAM RECALL: "Dream recall is always better in the hypnotic than in the waking state" (R. H. Rhodes, *Hypnosis: Theory, Practice and Application*).

DREAM WORK: The way in which dreams are formed as well as the elements contributing to their composition. Most prominent among these elements are: memories, emotions and wishes.

DROWSINESS: Traditionally, the hypnotists contended that hypnosis should be preceded by drowsiness, on the assumption that hypnosis is a kind of "sleep," but now it has been demonstrated (by W. R. Wells, for instance, in his article on "Experiments on Waking Hypnosis," in the *Journal of Abnormal and Social Psychology*, 1924) that drowsiness is not a pre-requisite of hypnosis.

DRUGS: "In some cases requiring medical treatment, drugs may be of valuable assistance, as facilitating the process of hypnotizing. Alcohol and also chloroform, chloral hydrate

(5 grains), paraldehyde (20mms.), veronal (½ grain), and cannabis indica (1½ grain) have been used with considerable success (by Esdaile, Schrenck-Notzing, Herrero, Bernheim, Jastrow, and others). All systematic use of chemicals should be discouraged, however, and the physician-hypnotist should resort to their application only in exceptional cases" (*Scientific Hypnotism*).

DURATION: The measured or estimated period of time. In the state of hypnosis it may be unrealistically lengthened or shortened.

E

ECHOLALIA: The tendency among hypnotized subjects to repeat, like phonographs, everything they hear, even what is said in foreign languages.

"The main point is that the hypnotic should know he is intended to repeat the sounds" (A. Moll, *Hypnotism*).

ECZEMA, see: *"Dermatosis."*

EDUCATION AND SUGGESTION: "Is it really incorrect to maintain that suggestion is one of the mighty tools of education, which can be used for good purposes and evil? Is it wrong to assert that no leadership is effective on a large scale, unless it resorts to suggestion?" (*Scientific Hypnotism*).

"Stage-fright is a psychological attitude affecting, and embarrassing to, many people. And consequently, hypnosis can be of help to: actors, singers, musicians, radio speakers, orators, lecturers, lawyers, students, etc. . . .

"Hypnosis can be, no doubt, successfully employed in teaching how to master the following skills: to swim, to skate, to ride a bicycle, to ride a horse, to drive a car, to dance, etc.

"I do not mean, of course, that hypnotic uggestion should be used in *all* instruction in the above activities. Quite the contrary, it should be resorted to only in *exceptional* cases, when a particular inability is clearly caused by a psychological attitude of fear and uncertainty and, consequently, by an inhibition. In fact, I do not recommend the application of hypnosis on a large scale. It should remain a powerful tool used with caution and discrimination" (*Ibid.*).

"A business man, in offering his products on the market, will not describe their qualities, good and bad, in an objective manner; rather, he will dwell on the attractive, exclusive, important features and thus try to arouse human attention and desire. A sign or a slogan does not impose, it suggests. And people yield to it, if it is built and presented according to the rules of popular psychology. These facts are appreciated in the business world to such an extent that, despite the colossal expense of education by advertising, no firm or industry can afford to neglect it" (*Ibid.*).

EIDETIC IMAGERY: Sensory imagery, primarily visual, which practically reaches the clarity of actual perception. It is fairly common in children and extremely rare in adults (except in sleep), but it can be readily aroused in hypnosis.

ELLIOTSON, JOHN (1791-1868): A British surgeon who came to use hypnosis (1837) as a kind of anaesthesia as well as a new treatment for nervous disorders. He also organized (1843) a magazine named *The Zoist* devoted to problems of unusual sort.

EMOTION: A state of feeling largely determined by specific experiences, but arising on the foundation of organic facilitation or inhibition. Accordingly, emotions result in increase or decrease of bodily activities. In consciousness, they may be classified as pleasant (e. g., joy) or unpleasant (e. g., disgust).

"Logical argumentation is powerless against effective interests. . . . The cleverest people suddenly behave as unintelligently as defectives as soon as their understanding encounters emotional resistance" (S. Freud, *Reflections on War and Death*).

"If we suppress either reason or emotion, we cramp both" (B. B. Wassell, *Group Psychoanalysis*).

"Emotion and suggestion are closely related. One commonly begets the other. Many emotional experiences, as is well known, have no clear source in the external conditions: they seem to be fully or partly imaginary. The fear of the dark, for instance, has no sufficient foundation, as a rule, for its existence in civilized conditions of life, as it had in the prehistoric days, when the darkness of the night concealed wild beasts and other dangerous enemies of man. Contempt and love are often inspired by persons and objects that are no more despicable or adorable, as the case may be, than other similar individuals and things. The emotion of love, particularly, is so permeated with products of imagination that it consists largely in creating illusions about the object of affection. Propaganda is known to arouse people to frenzy and worship, yet it attains its ends not so much through the study

35

or selection of facts as through utilizing the technique of suggestion and auto-suggestion" (*Scientific Hypnotism*).

"Pleasurable emotions promote and painful or disagreeable emotions depress the visceral functions" (A. Kunitz, *The Autonomic Nervous System*).

ENCEPHALOGRAPHY: The technique of recording bio-electrical activity of the human brain.

"The hypnotic sleep of a normal person is characterized by a gradual decrease of electric activity in the brain which, in itself, depends on the depth of hypnotic sleep" (M. P. Nevsky, in the *Psychotherapy in the Soviet Union*).

ESDAILE, JAMES (1808-1859) of Edinburgh: Having heard, while in Calcutta, of the anaesthetic use of hypnosis, he turned to it "to relieve the pain of a Hindu convict who was about to undergo a painful operation. The patient fell into a deep trance and felt no pain throughout the operation. Within several months he reported 75 successful and painless operations, and in the next three years he performed some 300 major operations and several thousand minor operations with uniformly painless results. This included nineteen amputations" (J. Stolzenberg, *Psychosomatics and Suggestion Therapy in Dentistry*).

EUPHORIA: A real or suggested state of high well-being.

EYEBALL SET TEST: When the subject is sitting and looking at the hypnotist, the latter starts talking as follows: "Sit comfortably and quietly. Close your eyes and try to turn the eyeballs upward, as if looking at something there. Then

36

shut your eyelids tighter and tighter and keep them that way. . . . Very good. It will be difficult to open them. One, two, three — you can't open them! Stop trying! . . . Now you can open your eyes."

If the subject is behaving as expected and follows every one of the hypnotist's instructions, he may be regarded as a cooperative and good subject.

F

FACILITATION: Increased ease of performing certain bodily activities as a result of suggestion or neural stimulation.

FAITH CURE: Auto-suggestion, which may assume the form of mass suggestion, probably underlies all cases of this sort. Moreover, healing of ailments without resort to drugs and surgery, is often connected with hysteria. It all largely depends on the person's mental attitude and may be facilitated by circumstances of his environment, social or otherwise.

FARIA, ABBÉ of Portugal: The author of *De la cause du sommeil lucide,* who came to Paris from India, and in

1814 arrived at the experimental conclusion that hypnosis has nothing to do with 'magnetism,' but is a psycho-physiological phenomenon rooted in suggestion.

FASCINATION: The method of hypnotizing by fixation of eyes on a small shining object held a little above the subject's eyes. This method was introduced by J. Braid. It is nowadays usually combined with verbal suggestion.

"I now proceed to detail the mode which I practice for producing the phenomena (of hypnosis). Take any bright object (I generally use my lancet case) between the thumb and fore and middle fingers of the left hand; hold it from about eight to fifteen inches from the eyes, at such position above the forehead as may be necessary to produce the greatest possible strain upon the eyes and eyelids, and enable the patient to maintain the steady fixed stare at the object. The patient must be made to understand that he is to keep the eyes steadily fixed on the object, and the mind riveted on the idea of that one object. It will be observed, that owing to the consensual adjustment of the eyes, the pupils will be at first contracted: they will shortly begin to dilate, and after they have done so to a considerable extent, and have assumed a wavy motion, if the fore and middle fingers of the right hand, extended and a little separated, are carried from the object towards the eyes, most probably the eyelids will close involuntarily" (James Braid, *Neurypnology*).

"I have seen that intense fixity of gaze sometimes induces hypnosis when other methods are useless, perhaps because the subjective expectation of the hypnosis is sooner aroused by the long, intense stare, than by verbal orders" (Albert Moll, *Hypnotism*).

FATHER HYPNOSIS: The authoritative technique of hypnotizing.

"We are inclined to believe that hypnotic submission is connected with willing obedience or even with paternal fixation. Apparently there are only two kinds of hypnosis: father-hypnosis (expressing submission to authority) and mother-hypnosis (expressing devotion)" (S. Ferenczi, *Further Contributions to the Theory and Technique of Psychoanalysis*).

FIXATION: Concentration of attention on a single sensation or object.

FLEXIBILITAS CEREA: In translation from Latin this means "waxy plasticity," or the subject's inclination to remain standing in whatever pose he is given by the hypnotist.

"In this condition a limb may be moulded into certain rather bizarre positions at the joints because of the great increase in relaxation of . . . muscles" (G. Ambrose and G. Newbold, *A Handbook of Medical Hypnosis*).

FOREL, AUGUST (1848-1931): Superintendent of the Zürich Lunatic Asylum in Switzerland, whose attempts to extend the use of hypnosis to medicine aroused much interest, particularly in Germany. He distinguished among three stages of hypnosis: drowsiness, hypotaxy and somnambulism.

"It is high time to stop doubting and procrastinating and to turn to a thorough study of the phenomena of hypnosis, which can extend our knowledge of psychology and of the physiology of the human brain. Medicine must not lag behind when such an opportunity presents itself" (August Forel's reply to Dr. K. A. Ewald's criticism).

41

FREE ASSOCIATION: Association of ideas formed in the absence of any outside interference or predisposing conditions. In psychoanalysis, it is a technique of treatment regarded as a means of access to the unconscious mind.

FREUD, SIGMUND (1856-1939): Born in Freiberg, Moravia, of Jewish parentage, he went to Vienna with his parents where he subsequently obtained medical education. He spent some time as a pupil of Charcot, got acquainted with Bernheim, and returned to Vienna to practice psychiatry. In the course of years he developed his own theory and technique of psychoanalysis. Among the best-known books of his are: *The Interpretation of Dreams, Introduction to Psychoanalysis, Psychopathology of Everyday Life, Civilization and Its Discontents,* and *Moses and Monotheism.* In 1909 he visited the United States, at the invitation of William James, and delivered a series of lectures at Clark University.

FRIGIDITY: The incapacity of some women to have a vaginal orgasm. It can be successfully treated in many cases by hypnosis or hypnoanalysis.
"It is fairly widespread among women in our Western civilization, and in most patients the symptom is characteristic of a psychosexual neurosis" (G. Ambrose and G. Newbold, *A Handbook of Medical Hypnosis*).

FUNCTIONAL DISORDERS: Disorders affecting bodily processes, the cause of which lies in mental pathology. Typical of these are some symptoms of hysteria, for instance, hysterical paralysis, blindness or deafness. Every one of these defects can be temporarily removed by suggestion or hypnosis. For permanent relief, however, the disease itself must be treated and eventually cured.

G

GAZE, FASCINATING, see: *"Fascination."*

GLOVE ANESTHESIA: A symptom of hysteria, in which the sensibility of the hand is lost. The deficiency can be readily overcome by hypnosis.

GROUP HYPNOSIS: "No hypnotist could meet a group of, say, thirty people and hypnotize the lot, unless . . . all thirty happened to be good subjects" (G. H. Estabrooks, *Hypnotism*).

GROUP PSYCHOTHERAPY: It can be used in two distinctive ways: either the group is treated by one hypnotist or the patients find themselves in an organized group of sympathetic persons of their own kind. The Alcoholics Anonymous illustrate the latter type of psychotherapy. Group hypnosis is rare in the countries of the Western world, but it has been extensively used by psychotherapists of the Soviet Union where they employ it in various connections, for instance, in the struggle against alcoholism.

"If psychotherapy is essentially a matter of teaching the patients how to live, why should we not teach them collectively in groups or classes as we teach dancing or chemistry or any other art or science, and by so doing reduce the cost of this much needed therapy to a point where people generally can take advantage of it? . . . I am convinced that it is not only the cheapest but also the most effective method to pursue" (Milton Harrington, *The Management of the Mind*).

"Group therapy has many advantages over individual treatment. For one thing, it permits an immense increase in the extent of medical service. It offers excellent opportunities for the physician to establish good contacts with his patients within a short period of time, thereby raising the chances of favorable developments. Explanatory talks conducted by the physician prove to be very convincing and are appreciated by the patients as providing serious scientific information rather than just routine consolation.

"In short, group psychotherapy makes it incomparably easier for the physician to put at the disposal of his patients various ways and means of counteracting and alleviating their own symptoms" (N. V. Ivanov, in the *Psychotherapy in the Soviet Union*).

H

HABIT FORMATION: A process of learning, partly conscious and partly unconscious, arising through repetition, usually in some acceptable form, whereby the response becomes fixed and almost automatic.

HALLUCINATE, TO: To have sense perceptions arising without any corresponding external stimulation.

HALLUCINATION: A sensory experience arising quite apart from any corresponding external stimulation. It is usually an indication of a psychosis, delirium or drug addiction. But it can also be produced as a test of hypnotic depth in perfectly normal people.

"In the visual domain, hallucination in the strict sense of the word is rarer than it is in the auditory domain. The difference doubtless depends upon the fact that the image of a noise is not absolutely contradicted by the sensation of a real noise, whereas a vision is often contradicted by the presence of the external objects amid which the vision seems to be situated. These objects then act as 'antagonistic reducers,' to use the term coined by Taine. I know perfectly well that two objects cannot occupy the same place at the same time, whereas two noises can mingle and interpenetrate" (Charles Baudouin, *Suggestion and Autosuggestion*).

"If told that he is standing on an iceberg at the North Pole, the subject will shiver with cold" (S. Edmunds, *Hypnotism and the Supernormal*).

HALLUCINATION, INDUCED, see: *"Induced Hallucination."*

HALLUCINATION, NEGATIVE: Strictly speaking, it is not a hallucination, for it refers to failure to observe realities, such as a door or the sound of a whistle. Nevertheless, this effect can be readily produced in persons under hypnosis. It is a kind of suggested inability to see or to hear certain things.

HALLUCINATION, RETROACTIVE: "Retroactive hallucinations are positive or negative, according as a new erroneous memory is created (by hypnosis) or an old one annulled. I say to a subject, 'You remember that we went to Potsdam yesterday, and took a drive on the Havel?' The suggestion takes effect, and the gentleman at once begins to relate his experiences in Potsdam. This is a retroactive positive hallucination. . . . The following would be a retroactive negative hallucination, as the hypnotic here forgets something which did happen: I say to him, 'You have not had any dinner; you have not had any breakfast.' Upon which he immediately feels hungry, as he thinks he has had nothing to eat since he got up" (A. Moll, *Hypnotism*).

HALLUCINOSIS: The state in which one has hallucinations as a result of mental or physical pathology, such as a psychosis, high fever, alcoholism, etc.

HAND CLASPING TEST: The subject is asked to look straight into the hypnotist's eyes while interlocking the fingers of both hands and pressing them tightly together. Then he is told that he cannot separate them, and if the subject is indeed unable to do so until the hypnotist commands him, he is regarded as ready for the proper treatment or else for an experiment.

HEMI-HYPNOSIS: A hypnotic state in which voluntary activities are confined to one side of the body as a result of hypnotic suggestion. To the same category of phenomena belongs also 'hemianesthesia' (loss of skin sensitivity on one side) and 'hemianopsia' (loss of vision on one side).

HETERO-HYPNOSIS: The usual form of hypnosis as opposed to auto-hypnosis.

HETERO-SUGGESTION: Suggestion the source of which lies in another person (called a hypnotist or operator) rather than in oneself.

"As Ernest Jones has said (in the *British Journal of Medi-*

cal Psychology, 1923), 'It is extraordinarily difficult to draw any sharp line between hetero- and auto-suggestion. . . .' It is not necessary, however, to believe that the source of auto-suggestion lies within the subject, whereas the source of hetero-suggestion resides solely in the operator. Even when one's mind appears to act spontaneously, external influences may play an important role; and when it seems to follow only the orders of another person, one's individual tendencies may be really responsible for the behavior. The entire controversy as to whether all auto-suggestion is actually hetero-suggestion, or vice versa, is futile, as both involve almost identical forces, though aroused in two different fashions" (*Scientific Hypnotism*).

HIGHER MENTAL PROCESSES: Power of thought and creative activities. According to C. Baudouin's observations, the quality of the subject's thought does not appear to be seriously affected by hypnosis, while imagination becomes often enhanced in vigor.

HULL, CLARK L. (1871-1955): The author of *Hypnosis and Suggestibility* (1933) was born in a log cabin and raised on a farm. In his educational advance, he was continually and seriously delayed by poor health, but he never gave up and eventually completed it at the University of Wisconsin and remained teaching there until he was called to Yale. His main interests lay in the theory of learning and suggestibility.

HYPERAESTHESIA: Extreme sharpness of the senses. Their increase in vigor can sometimes be achieved under the influence of hypnotic suggestion, whether it be sight, hearing or taste.

HYPERMNESIA: An unusual ability to retain or recall. It can often be demonstrated and further increased by means of hypnosis. It can then be used "to recover memories of very early childhood which might reasonably be presumed to have been lost through the ordinary processes of forgetting" (C. L. Hull, *Hypnosis and Suggestibility*).

HYPERSUGGESTIBILITY: Heightened suggestibility characteristic of deep hypnosis.
"Hypnotist . . . facilitates suggestion" (H. M. Bernheim, *Suggestive Therapeutics*).

HYPERSUGGESTIBILITY, HETEROACTIVE: Slight increase in the subject's suggestibility, characteristic of series of hypnotic sessions in which the procedure is altered each time.

HYPERSUGGESTIBILITY, HOMOACTIVE: Marked increase in suggestibility caused by each preceding hypnotic session, insofar as the same procedure is followed.

HYPNAGOGIC: Inducing sleep; hypnotic.

HYPNIC: Pertaining to sleep; hypnotic.

HYPNOANALYSIS: The practice of psychoanalysis conducted under hypnosis (initiated by J. A. Hadfield). It was successfully used during the Second World War. The time required for treatment can be considerably shortened in this way, as compared to traditional psychoanalysis.
"In hypnoanalysis, the patient is seen five or six times a week for a few months. The first fifteen minutes of each hypnoanalytic session may be devoted to orthodox free associa-

49

tion. The patient is then put in a deep trance and given various suggestions to stimulate the recall of repressed or early experiences. The analyst may ask the hypnotized patient to report free associations, relate suggested dreams, relive and reenact emotional scenes, report what he sees in a crystal ball, and so on. In brief, the analyst acts as a guide leading the hypnotized patient through a maze of unconscious material" (J. B. Page, *Abnormal Psychology*).

"Hypnosis does add an element of speed to therapy, without altering its dynamics" (A. Kardiner, quoted in L. R. Wolberg's *Hypnoanalysis*).

HYPNOANALYST: The psychiatrist using the combination of psychoanalysis and hypnosis.

HYPNODIAGNOSIS: The use of hypnosis for the purpose of identifying the subject's needs or difficulties and of facilitating psychological testing and diagnosis.

HYPNODONTICS: A new variety of dentistry, which uses hypnosis.

"The mere handling of patients on a somatic basis, in itself, is very vexing. There is no question that patients will find it more pleasurable to spend their time, either in the barber chair or in the chair of a beauty salon, in preference to a session in the dental chair. As for children, there is no question that they will find a great deal more pleasure at play rather than in a dental office. However, it is a necessary part of our functional mechanism to enjoy the benefits of good teeth, both from a functional and aesthetic point of view. Dental services rendered to patients can be made more acceptable by the application of suggestion, whether it be in the form of conscious suggestion or by hypnosis" (J.

Stolzenberg, *Psychosomatics and Suggestion Therapy in Dentistry*).

HYPNOGENIC: Producing sleep or hypnosis.

HYPNOIDAL: Resembling hypnosis; characterized by a very light form of it.

HYPNOLOGY: Study of sleep or hypnosis.

HYPNONARCOSIS: A state of deep sleep induced through hypnosis.

HYPNOPLASTY: Modelling clay in the hypnotic state.

HYPNORELAXATION: Suggestive treatment seeking relief from anxiety and other tension states.

HYPNOSIS: The state or condition induced through effective suggestion or the method of doing so. The subject may be placed in a reclining position and told to follow the hypnotist's instructions. The purpose of this is to obtain a trance-like state resembling sleep, in which the subject manifests readiness to react to the hypnotist's voice. This ability often exceeds anything that can be done in the ordinary waking state and may include some physiological changes, particularly inhibition.

"A patient may be hypnotized by keeping the eyes fixed in *any* direction. It occurs most *slowly* and *feebly* when the eyes are directed straight forward, and most *rapidly* and *intensely* when they can be maintained in the position of a double internal and upward squint" (James Braid, *Neurypnology*).

"Hypnosis is a form of 'partial sleep of the hemispheres' " (I. P. Pavlov, in the *Scientific Monthly,* 1923).

"The command to sleep in hypnosis means nothing more or less than an order to withdraw all interest from the world and to concentrate it upon the person of the hypnotist. And it is so understood by the subject; for in this withdrawal of interest from the outer world lies the psychological characteristic of sleep, and the kinship between the sleep and the state of hypnosis is based upon it" (Sigmund Freud, *Group Psychology and the Analysis of the Ego*).

"Hypnosis is an aspect of the conditioned reflex, probably the most undeniable fact of modern psychology" (Andrew Salter, *What Is Hypnosis*).

"Hypnosis is the production of reactions in the human organism through the use of verbal and other associative reflexes" (*Ibid.*).

"Such words as 'splendid,' 'marvelous,' and 'magnificent' give us an unconscious lift because we have been conditioned to that feeling in them" (*Ibid.*).

"The use of hypnosis in therapy requires as much training, background, and knowledge as any other form of psychotherapy" (A. M. Weitzenhoffer, in the *Annual Review of Hypnosis Literature,* 1950-51).

"There are few medical conditions indeed in which hypnotism cannot be usefully employed either as the main treatment or a valuable auxiliary" (S. J. Van Pelt, in the *Medical Hypnosis Handbook*).

"It is as a means of shortening treatment that hypnosis is of value" (W. Moodie, *Hypnosis in Treatment*).

"Hypnosis is no panacea, but only one of the most effective

52

methods of acting upon the patient's organism through the higher centers of his nervous system — his cortex" (M. M. Zheltakov, in the *Psychotherapy in the Soviet Union*).

HYPNOSIS BY PHONOGRAPH RECORDS, see: *"Recording, Phonograph or Tape."*

HYPNOSIS, DEEP, see: *"Stuporous Trance."*

HYPNOSYNTHESIS: Integration of unbearable dissociated experiences by means of hypnosis.

HYPNOTARIUM: A slightly darkened room in a hospital or sanatorium, specifically organized for hypnotic treatments in groups of four or five patients suffering from an identical illness, such as alcoholism or hysteria.

HYPNOTHERAPY: Medical or psychiatric treatment by means of hypnosis, occasionally combined with some form of re-education.

"For the successful practice of hypnotherapy, a strong, firm, positive and reassuring approach is a *sine qua non* (S. J. Van Pelt, in the *Medical Hypnosis Handbook*).

"It is well known among professional people that there are two main forms of hypnosis. One is inseparable from an emotional attitude toward the hypnotist who becomes the source of overpowering stimulations comparable to strong sounds or bright lights. The other form of hypnosis has the opposite effect: it pacifies, makes one sleepy. In all this, the hypnotist and his words remain the only link between the patient and the outside world — indeed, the only directive force" (V. N. Miassischev, in the *Psychotherapy in the Soviet Union*).

HYPNOTIC: I. *Adj.* Pertaining to sleep or hypnosis. II. *Noun.* A person in the hypnotic state. See: *"Subject."*

HYPNOTIC SLEEP, see: *"Sleep, Hypnotic."*

HYPNOTIC STATE: "The hypnotic state is essentially a state of mental concentration, in which the faculties of the mind of the patient are so engrossed with a single idea or train of thought as, for the nonce, to be dead or indifferent to all other considerations and influences" (James Braid, *Neurypnology*).

"An extensive series of experiments has failed to find a physiological index which differentiates 'the hypnotic state' from 'the waking state.' " (T. X. Barber, in the *Psychological Bulletin,* 1961).

"The hypnotic state is a prestige-and-faith relationship in which the practitioner uses his advantageous position to influence by suggestion the subject's autonomic nervous system, in order to effect desired bodily inhibitions and excitations and to condition his mind accordingly" (*Scientific Hypnotism*).

HYPNOTISM: The field as well as the theory and practice of hypnosis for the purposes of scientific study, experimentation and treatment. The term, coined by James Braid in 1843, should not be used as synonymous with 'hypnosis,' the latter referring to the state induced in a subject.

The British Medical Association accepted the hypnotic method of treatment as valuable in psychiatry (1892) and a similar decision was made in Paris, France, by the International Congress of Hypnotism in 1900.

HYPNOTISM ACT, THE: This act of British legislation (1952) concerns the right of local authorities to grant licenses, under certain conditions, to regulate or prohibit public demonstrations of hypnosis. Any person guilty of such demonstration of hypnosis without a license and involving a person or persons under the age of twenty-one is liable on summary conviction to a fine not exceeding fifty pounds. This Act does *not* prevent the use of hypnosis for scientific purposes or for the treatment of mental or physical diseases. The Act has come into force on April 1, 1953, and applies to the British Isles with the exception of Northern Ireland.

HYPNOTIST: The person conducting scientific experiments or treatment by means of hypnosis.

"Being a hypnotist is a specialist's job" (S. Edmunds, *Hypnotism and the Supernormal*).

HYPNOTIZABILITY, see: *"Suggestibility."*

HYPNOTIZE, TO: To put a subject or subjects into the state of hypnosis.

HYPNOTIZER, see: *"Hypnotist."*

HYPOGALACTIA: Insufficiency of milk in the mother's breasts at the time of her baby's birth.

James Braid "hypnotized a patient who was nursing, and suggested an increased secretion of milk in one breast. On awaking she had no recollection of what had been done, but complained of a feeling of tightness and tension in the breast. Her husband then told her that Braid had been trying to increase the secretion of milk. She was sceptical as to the result, as the child was fourteen months old and the milk had almost disappeared. Her breast, however, almost immediately became distended with milk, and a few days later she complained that her figure was deformed in consequence. Braid again hypnotized her and successfully repeated the experiment with the other breast. The patient suckled her child for six months longer, the supply of milk being more abundant than it had been at any time since her confinement" (as reported in J. M. Bramwell's *Hypnotism*).

HYPOTAXY: In the terminology of A. Forel, this is the middle stage of hypnosis in which the subject's eyes are already closed and he generally obeys suggestions. It is usually preceded by the stage of drowsiness and may be followed by that of somnambulism.

HYSTERIA: A mental disease, usually classified as one of the neuroses. The very variety of observable symptoms of this disease indicates that it is connected with high defensive suggestibility. By a kind of organic 'pretense,' it may assume a form of blindness, deafness, paralysis, loss of memory, etc., or else may result in strange forms of behavior including sleepwalking, fugue or mutism.

I

IATROGENY: Undesirable neurotic effects, usually un-intentional, of a physician's words or activities upon his sub-ject. The effect is in a way natural, sometimes unavoidable, insofar as the diagnosis of a serious or lasting disease, chance of death, or need for an expensive operation may indeed be shocking.

"The victims of iatrogenic neuroses are mainly persons with nerve weakness" (M. A. Zhilinskaya and L. G. Pervov, in the *Psychotherapy in the Soviet Union*).

IDEOMOTOR SIGNAL, see: *"Signal, Ideomotor."*

IDEOPLASTY: The process of making the subject's mind plastic and receptive by means of useful and attractive ideas suggested by the hypnotist.

ILLUSION: Misinterpretation of certain phenomena as a result of misleading or suggestive features of the situation. All kinds of illusions can be readily suggested to the subject in the state of hypnosis, provided they are compatible with his personality and moral beliefs.

IMAGINATION: Constructive reorganization of sensory or ideational data of experience. A subject in the hypnotic state is very susceptible to accept or even to create them in a vivid way.

IMPOTENCE: Male inability to perform sexual intercourse. It can often be treated successfully by hypnosis.

INDIVIDUAL PSYCHOLOGY: A variety of psychoanalysis developed by Alfred Adler (1870-1937), an Austrian psychiatrist, founded on the technique of reducing feelings of inferiority.

INDUCED HALLUCINATION: Hallucination formed in a subject's mind as a result of a hypnotic suggestion. Such a hallucination serves as a test of depth of the hypnotic state.

INDUCTION, see: *"Trance Induction."*

INDUCTION TECHNIQUES, see: *"Methods of Inducing Hypnosis."*

INHIBITION: Organic prevention of certain bodily activities or modes of expression as a result of an inner conflict of emotions or motives. It may be caused by interference with natural impulses or by unwelcome outside pressures.

"Inhibition, ordinary sleep and hypnosis are one and the same process. . . ." Inhibition is "sleep distributed in localized parts" (I. P. Pavlov, in the *Scientific Monthly*, 1923).

"The rapidity with which the subject will demonstrate inhibition and excitation and changes in the bodily state produced by hypnosis demonstrate the activity of the autonomic nervous system and its neural pathways" (J. Stolzenberg, *Psychosomatics and Suggestion Therapy in Dentistry*).

INSOMNIA: Sleeplessness for emotional or psychological reasons.

"In the control of insomnia, which is more often due to faulty psychological patterns than to disturbed physiological processes, autohypnosis has been effective" (R. H. Rhodes, *Therapy through Hypnosis*).

J

JANET, PIERRE (1859-1947): French psychiatrist influenced, during the early years of his career, by J. M. Charcot. But subsequently he turned toward a more objective interpretation of psychiatry and developed his theory of dissociation in a series of important volumes (see: *"Dissociation."*).

JUNG, CARL GUSTAV (1875-1946): A Swiss psychiatrist, originally a close associate of Sigmund Freud, who subsequently formed his own school of thought known as Analytical Psychology and built around the "racial unconscious," or the pattern of mind reflecting primitive and somewhat morbid tendencies exemplified by the following quotation from his *Modern Man in Search of a Soul*:

"I am convinced that it is hygienic to discover in death a goal towards which we can strive, and that shrinking from it is something unhealthy and abnormal which robs the second half of life of its purpose."

K

KNEE-JERK: M. J. Bass' experiments have clearly demonstrated that the state of hypnosis (specifically, somnambulism) is physiologically different from that of ordinary sleep. The investigation was conducted with subjects in a reclining position, who were given altogether 12,900 patellar stimulations. The results of the experiments have shown that the knee-jerk in the state of trance is very similar to that of the waking state, whereas a sleeping subject manifests a totally different and much smaller reflex.

L

LEARNED SOCIETIES AND ORGANIZATIONS (in the field of hypnotism):

The American Society of Clinical Hypnosis (Member Organization of the World Federation for Mental Health and Affiliate of the American Association for the Advancement of Science). Address: 800 Washington Ave., S. E., Minneapolis, Minn.

It has numerous component sections, namely:

Akron	Greater St. Louis	Northeast Alabama
Alamo	Houston	Northeastern N. Y.
Alberta Academy	Kansas	Philadelphia
Arkansas	Luzerne County, Pa.	Puerto Rico
Ark.-La.-Tex.	Magic Valley	San Diego
Central Ohio	Maine	San Francisco
Chicago	Memphis	San Jose
Dallas	Metropolitan N. Y.	Springfield, Mass.
Dist. of Columbia	Michigan	Tucson
Finger Lakes	Nebraska	Virginia
Georgia	New England	Western Pennsylvania
Greater Kansas City	New Jersey	Youngstown

Education and Research Foundation, established and controlled by ASCH for the purpose of conducting charitable, educational, and scientific activities by qualified persons in medicine, dentistry, psychology, and related fields. Address: 800 Washington Ave., S. E., Minneapolis, Minn.

The International Congresses on Hypnosis. The first Congress of this kind took place in Paris, August, 1889; it was attended, among others, by S. Freud, P. Janet, J. M. Charcot, H. M. Bernheim, and A. A. Liébeault. In our own days, the idea was revived when another Congress met in New York City on November 18th and 19th, 1961.

LETHARGY: A stage of hypnosis characterized by general anesthesia and muscular flaccidity. In a broader sense, it is deep sleep or stupor.

LIÉBEAULT, A. A. (1823-1904): The founder of the therapeutics of suggestion and author of *Du sommeil* (1866) who established (with H. M. Bernheim) the School of Nancy and whose method depended upon mild and monotonous stimulation. The purpose of this was "to tire the senses of the subject" so as to make him feel "a desire to rest, to sleep, to submit, to acquiesce" (S. L. Krebs, *The Fundamental Principles of Hypnosis*).

LIMEN: Threshold of stimulation; the minimal intensity of it required to initiate a nerve impulse.

LIMINAL SENSITIVITY (LS): The lowest intensity of stimulation that gives rise to a particular sensation.

LUYS METHOD: Dr. J. Luys (the latter part of the 19th Century), member of the French Academy of Medicine and the head of the Hospital de la Charité in Paris, tried to combine and reconcile all the available techniques of hypnotizing. But at the core of his method really lay a very ingenious device called "mirror rotatif," consisting of two mirrors revolving in opposite directions. By gazing at this contraption and simultaneously listening to the hypnotist, the patient found his eyes quickly fatigued and himself ready for hypnosis.

"Many advantages are claimed for this method — that it saves the operator time and trouble, and is impersonal; that a number of people can be hypnotized at the same time by its means; and that it never fails" (R. H. Vincent, *The Elements of Hypnotism*).

M

MAGNETISM, ANIMAL, see: *"Animal Magnetism."*

MEDICAL HYPNOSIS: Hypnosis used by a qualified physician for a medical purpose.

"Relaxation, realization and re-education may be regarded as the three R's of hypno-suggestive therapy" (S. J. Van Pelt, in the *Medical Hypnosis Handbook*).

"How much suffering could have been prevented if the patient had thought of hypnosis first, instead of 'as a last resort'!" (*Ibid.*).

"Suggestion does not perform miracles, let it be understood once and for all. It is completely helpless in maladies rooted in anatomical defects or in physiological troubles basically independent of the involuntary system. It is, indeed, foolish to hope that hypnosis will cure diphtheria, syphilis, or appendicitis. Fully recognizing these obvious limitations, we should not at the same time forget that there exist cases, quite numerous in fact, in which the symptom has merely the appearance of an anatomical defect, as in hysterical blindness, deafness or paralysis. The physician should remain strictly scientific in his diagnosis and know how to differentiate between these psychic ailments and similar organic maladies that require ordinary surgery or are totally incurable" (*Scientific Hypnotism*).

MEMORY: Human ability to retain information, to recall past experiences, and to gain in skills.
"With hypnotism we can cut out entire memories for certain events which have taken place in past years" (G. H. Estabrooks, *Hypnotism*).
"Patients under hypnosis show a remarkable ability to bring up material that they do not remember consciously" (L. R. Wolberg, *Hypnoanalysis*).

MESMER, FRANZ ANTON (1734-1815): A native of Switzerland, he went to Austria to earn his medical degree and obtained it by writing his thesis on the topic of "De Planetarium Influxu," in which he postulated the existence of a magnetic fluid which pervaded the whole world and, under certain conditions, could be used to produce remarkable effects upon the human body and mind. After some experimentation with hypnosis (1775), he left Vienna and went to Paris, where he formulated the theory of animal magnetism (1779) and turned to group therapy around his "baquet" (*see*), which soon proved to be so successful as to arouse much jealousy among local physicians. As a result, all kinds of rumors spread and the French government found it advisable to appoint a Royal Commission to investigate the case, which included some scientists, among them Benjamin Franklin and Lavoisier. The Commission arrived at the conclusion that there actually was no evidence of any 'magnetic fluid' and that, consequently, the cures were misrepresented. As a result, Mesmer had to discontinue his luxurious practice, went to Germany and died there in obscurity.

MESMERISM: The technique of hypnotizing developed by F. A. Mesmer in accordance with his theory of animal magnetism. See: *"Animal Magnetism."*

MESMERIZE, TO: To hypnotize, particularly in the manner practiced by F. A. Mesmer.

METHODS OF INDUCING HYPNOSIS: There are now no prescribed methods of hypnotizing, except that they all should conform to the rules of professional ethics. The field is still wide open, in this respect, for research in scientific methodology. But, except for mesmerism, which has been completely discredited, history has much to offer for information and reasonable choice, as shown by the following examples:

Mesmer: Fundamentally, his method depended on the credulity of men who would be impressed by the strange environment in which he worked — as strange as his own sincere beliefs in animal magnetism. But he apparently succeeded in conveying to his patients the idea of controlling forces of nature and human health by using downward contact passes, from shoulders to finger tips. Anyway, many of his patients were cured, and others felt better.

Esdaile: He was of the opinion that both hypnosis and sleep were states of relaxation, with one significant difference — that, in the former instance, the power of suggestion could gain control of the subject's mind and even of his body, as in the case of surgery made painless. To put the subject into the state of hypnosis, it seemed advisable, therefore, to promote conditions of normal sleep, that is, to make him close his eyes and relax in bed, to darken the room, while carrying on a steady stream of appropriate verbal suggestions.

Braid: The physical aspect of hypnosis was subordinated by him to the mental one, insofar as he recognized that, if suggestions are to be effective at all, the subject's attention must be guided to concentrate on a single idea. This he sought to achieve through the technique of fascination, in which the patient was enabled to relax and concentrate his attention on a bright object, such as a lancet-case, thus allowing a succession of suggestions to enter his mind unobstructed and unresisted.

Liébeault: He preferred to place the patient in an armchair rather than on a bed and to make him look straight into his own eyes, so as to divert the subject's attention from the essence of his suggestions. When the subject's eyes became clearly tired, he would utter several times the suggestion of "Your eyes are getting heavy, your limbs feel numb, and you become more and more drowsy." The subject usually promptly reacted by entering the state of hypnosis and was able to undergo whatever treatment was indicated for him.

Bernheim: As a partner of Liébeault in the School of Nancy, he employed essentially the same technique of hypnotic induction as stated in the preceding paragraph. At the same time, to avoid any chance of uneasiness or worry on the patient's part, he preferred to begin the first session with a clear and calming explanation of the entire procedure and to add a few words concerning the therapeutic value of suggestion.

See also: *"Auto-Hypnosis," "Donatism," "Hypnoanalysis."*

MIGRAINE: A form of headache, periodic in nature. It is often preceded by an optic aura, may be limited to one side, and commonly ends in nausea or vomiting. It is usually emotional in origin. If approached in the spirit of personality re-education, it can be effectively treated by hypnosis.

MIMICRY, UNCONSCIOUS: Involuntary activities of the subject, particularly in the facial expression, reflecting the mental contents of the moment. Experiments have demonstrated that this may also be suggested by hypnosis.

MIND AND BODY: "There is a power of mind over body that cannot be denied. It used to be conceived as a mystical influence of the disembodied soul upon mortal flesh. Science offers us a more reliable explanation. We observed that, under the pressure of a powerful and appropriate suggestion, almost any part of the organism may begin to act in a fashion which under no circumstance can be reproduced at will. It does not matter whether the change takes place under hypnosis or in an ordinary waking state. In either case suggestion is operative. In fact, many of the phenomena commonly observed under hypnosis have also been seen apart from it, in the normal state of high suggestibility, or in the abnormal state of hysteria. The question that stands before us is then: What is the bodily mechanism underlying these phenomena?" (*Scientific Hypnotism*).

"A number of years ago, I entered a grocery store to buy a few tomatoes, my favorite vegetable. As I was selecting

73

them, I happened to turn over one large tomato, right in time to see a large, fat worm crawl out of it. It was silly, of course, to allow myself to be influenced by this sight — I did not buy *that* tomato, after all — but the fact remains that I could not eat any tomatoes that day and for the subsequent year. The mere sight of tomatoes would invariably bring back the recollection . . . and disgust. Even today I have not completely regained my former predilection for the vegetable. . . .

"A somewhat more striking case was reported to me by a student of mine, which I shall relate in his own words: 'One of my friends desired to learn to read the medical thermometer. I inserted an oral thermometer into his mouth in order that his temperature might be recorded. It remained there for about a minute when I told him that he was using a rectal thermometer. He became very much excited. In a few seconds he began to vomit profusely.' I do not recall the purpose of this experiment; perhaps, there was none. But even if it was merely a practical joke, the student surely should be forgiven, for the sake of science.

"Such everyday instances are familiar to most of us and could be multiplied without end. The trained nurses know that a patient, after several weeks of periodical morphine injections, will feel genuine relief from his pains when simple water is injected hypodermically, provided he does not suspect the substitution of the drug. Rashes have been known to break out, only as a result of apprehension that one had contracted some contagious disease or had handled poison ivy. People commonly develop sea-sickness *before* the boat has actually left the harbor. Fear of the dark is likely to accelerate the heart beat, even though the terrors of night are purely imaginary" (*Ibid.*)

MONOIDEISM: James Braid's finding that the state of hypnosis depends on the narrowing or limiting of the subject's attention.

MOTHER HYPNOSIS: The coaxing technique of hypnotizing. See: *"Father Hypnosis."*

N

NAIL-BITING: A habit rooted in insecurity and arising usually during adolescence. It can be readily handled by hypnosis, but it requires some psychiatric help for permanent cure.

"The problem is primarily that of transforming without attacking" (M. H. Erickson, S. Hershman, and I. I. Secter, *The Practical Application of Medical and Dental Hypnosis*).

NANCY SCHOOL: A research and hypnotic treatment center founded in the city of Nancy, France, by A. A. Liébeault (1866) who was joined later by H. M. Bernheim. It was run on the assumption that hypnosis is a powerful form of normal suggestion. The specific method of hypnotizing was described as follows:

"The patient is comfortably seated in an easy chair with his back to the light, and the operator stands by his side, holding up two fingers of his own hand some few inches from the patient's eyes. The patient is told to look intently at these two fingers, and as far as possible to keep his mind a blank. As soon as the eyes begin to show symptoms of weariness, the hypnotist begins in a somewhat muffled and monotonous tone of voice to suggest sleep. Sometimes the operator, without waiting for the symptoms to appear, will start at once telling the patient, 'You are beginning to feel drowsy;' 'Your sight is getting dim,' etc." (R. H. Vincent, *The Elements of Hypnotism,* 1897).

NARCO-ANALYSIS: Hypnoanalysis combined with the use of light narcosis in difficult cases.

"Some patients who resist deep trance states enter somnambulism states easily under the influence of hypnotic drugs" (L. R. Wolberg, *Hypnoanalysis*).

"Suggestible patients become more suggestible after injection of sodium amytal in subanaesthetic doses" (H. J. Eysenck and W. L. Reed, in the *Journal of Mental Science,* 1945).

NARCOSYNTHESIS: Restoration and re-living of memories (lost as a result of shell-shock and other damages to the brain) by means of narcotic drugs, such as sodium pentothal. The technique was developed by R. R. Grinker and J. P. Spiegel during the Second World War.

NEGATIVE HALLUCINATION, see: *"Hallucination, Negative."*

NEGATIVE HYPNOSIS, see: *"Hypnosis, Negative."*

NEGATIVE SUGGESTIBILITY, see: *"Suggestibility, Negative."*

NEGATIVISIM: Resistance to suggestions to the extent of taking the opposite course of action; such behavior is sometimes called 'active negativism.' When it is confined to refusal to conform, it is called 'passive negativism.'

NERVOUS SLEEP: J. Braid's descriptive term for hypnosis.

NEURASTHENIA: G. M. Beard's term (1880) for emotional disturbance in reaction to personal problems and difficulties, which may end in chronic nervous prostration. Professional treatment by hypnosis results in the recovery of about 30% of all cases, as reported by H. M. Bernheim, J. Bramwell, A. Forel, von Schrenck-Nothing, O. G. Wetterstrand, and many others.

NEURODERMATITIS: Inflammation of the skin, of neurotic origin. See: *"Dermatosis."*

NEUROSIS: A functional disorder of the nervous system; professionally it is distinguished from psychosis in which some physical or chemical cause is responsible for the illness.

"Hypnosis is valuable only in neuroses of fairly recent origin, where the immediate cause of the symptoms is known. If a symptom is based on a neurotic personality, the cure is only temporary" (R. W. Nice, *A Handbook of Abnormal Psychology*).

NEUROTIC: A person afflicted with a neurotic condition. "The neurotic's demands for love are so insatiable that they cannot be fullfilled in reality" (L. R. Wolberg, *Hypnoanalysis*).

NEURYPNOLOGY, see: *"Braidism."*

NIGHT WALKING, see: *"Somnambulism."*

NOCTAMBULISM, see: *"Somnambulism."*

O

OBSESSION: A driving, sometimes irresistible, idea; when combined with an emotion, it is likely to result in action, sometimes endlessly repeated. Obsessions have been classified under the following headings: intellectual, inhibiting, and compulsive.

OCCUPATIONAL THERAPY: A method of treatment for the hospitalized sick, injured or weak, which protects them from boredom, serves as a kind of entertainment, provides stimulating social intercourse, and in some instances prepares them for useful activity in the outside world. To get the maximum benefit out of such therapy, it may be desirable to combine it with hypnotic treatments.

ONEIROSIS: A form of light hypnosis resembling som-nolence ('oneiros' means dream in Greek) rather than sleep ('hypnos,' sleep).

"As soon as the subject is informed, in the pre-hypnotic stage, that he is going to be aware of everything that happens to him in the trance, that he will subsequently recall distinctly his experiences in the state, and that the state will end immediately upon command, he is sincerely ready for cooperation. . . .

"Few people are ever annoyed by the state of hypnosis in general, but in reports on oneirosis the expressions of surprise and pleasure are particularly common. 'It was a very enjoyable and agreeable state,' writes one. 'I felt like remaining that way for a long time,' confesses another. 'I did not want to come out of the state,' asserts the third. 'There seemed to be one thing that held my attention; it was the warm, joyous blood in my veins,' states the fourth.

"Let me cite a more detailed passage from one of my subject's reports: 'There is no other state comparable to it. It is somewhat between a waking and a sleeping state — a drowsy, comfortable inertia envelops one. Regardless of the position taken, whether sitting, slouching, or reclining, during the state I feel utterly at ease. I have never had the desire to awaken nor to fall asleep — merely to continue in that state. There is no consciousness of the body, of the chair, of the room, of anything except the voice, speaking, speaking, speaking. Under the state I am conscious of nothing, yet acutely aware of everything. The tick of the clock, the dropping of a pin, the window shade moving, the opening of the door . . . no change in the environment escapes me'." (*Scientific Hypnotism*).

OPERATOR, see: *"Hypnotist."*

P

PAIN: An unpleasant sensation, the biological significance of which lies in the drive of avoidance, just as the significance of pleasure lies in the drive of approach, continuation or repetition.

"Our entire psychic activity is bent upon producing pleasure and avoiding pain" (S. Freud, *A General Introduction to Psychoanalysis*).

PAINLESS BIRTH, see: *"Childbirth."*

PARALYSIS, HYPNOTIC: A temporary loss of motor function in some part of the body as a result of hypnotic suggestion.

PASSES: Sweeping motions with the arms, presumably helpful in trance induction.

"The passes with contact act in exactly the same way as the passes without contact. In any case — and this is important — the effect only appears when the individual has an idea of what is intended to follow" (A. Moll, *Hypnotism*).

PAVLOV, IVAN P. (1849-1936): The famous Russian physiologist and psychologist, best known for his theory of conditioned reflexes, for which he received the Nobel Prize (1904). He regarded the phenomena of hypnosis as a form of partial sleep of the two hemispheres of the brain.

"In the animal, the sense of reality is indicated almost exclusively by stimulations and by the traces they leave in the cerebral hemispheres, which come directly to the special cells of the visual, auditory or other receptors of the organism. This is what we, too, receive as sensations, impressions and notions of the world around us, both the natural and the social, with the exception of words heard or seen. The former system of signals is common to men and animals. But speech constitutes a second signal system which is peculiarly ours" (*Lectures on Conditioned Reflexes*).

PHOBIA: Overwhelming pathological fear of a particular kind, exemplified by acrophobia, fear of high places, or nyctophobia, fear of darkness.

PHONOGRAPH RECORDS, see: *"Records, Phonograph or Tape."*

PHRENOMAGNETISM: The hypothetical power of stimulating the brain through the use of mesmerism.

PHYSIOLOGY OF HYPNOSIS: According to medical authorities, the physiology of hypnosis, including reflex activities, brain waves, and the psycho-galvanic reflex, is basically identical with that of the waking rather than the sleeping state.

POSITIVE SUGGESTION: "The prevailing tendency among hypnotists to stress muscular and sensory inhibitions — *not* to move this limb or that, *not* to see this object, *not* to hear that sound, *not* to feel any pain — serves largely to conceal from scientific attention the vast field of positive suggestion. It consists in stimulating, rather than in inhibiting, various bodily and mental functions, as well as in removing undesirable inhibitions. Positive suggestion cannot always rely on mechanical obedience of the subject, which is usually connected with somnambulism. It often calls for an intense activity of the mind, in recalling forgotten experiences, in imagining new sensations, in reasoning out problems, and in establishing fresh forms of emotional conditioning. These purposes are promoted by the clearness of the subject's mind. He manifests a better response in a light trance" (*Scientific Hypnotism*).

POST-HYPNOTIC AMNESIA, see: "*Amnesia, Post-Hypnotic.*"

POST-HYPNOTIC SUGGESTION: Suggestion given by the hypnotist to his subject to be carried out subsequently, in the waking state.
"The expression, 'post-hypnotic suggestion,' is somewhat misleading. Really it refers not to suggestions given after the trance, but to those offered during it to be executed subsequently" (*Scientific Hypnotism*).

"Whenever the subject must be hypnotized repeatedly, it is always desirable to shorten the pre-hypnotic period. The procedure becomes easier with every sitting. But it will be truly of negligible duration, if the operator tells his subject, just before arousing him from the preceding trance, to enter the state practically instantaneously at the next sitting. As a result, it sometimes suffices to snap the fingers, and the subject is immediately in the trance" (*Ibid.*).

POSTURAL SWAY TEST: A test of hypnotic readiness. The subject is asked to stand on both feet placed together, to look straight forward, and to stare fixedly at something slightly above his eyes, while the hypnotist stands squarely behind and begins to rock him slightly. Then the hypnotist tells the subject that the latter feels being strongly drawn backward. When the subject loses his balance, he is caught by the supporting hands.

PRE-HYPNOTIC SUGGESTION: "We can also distinguish another kind of suggestion: something may be suggested to the subject before the hypnosis which is to follow in that state. This is pre-hypnotic suggestion" (A. Moll, *Hypnotism*).

PRESTIGE: Professional or public recognition of one's ability and skill in a specialized field or in general; good reputation. Prestige of a hypnotist happens to be, in addition, of considerable value in reducing difficulties in trance induction.

PRESTIGE-AND-FAITH RELATION: The proper relation between the subject and the hypnotist. Skeptics as well as relatives and friends should be allowed to see at least one person hypnotized before they are accepted as subjects themselves.

PRESTIGE SUGGESTION: Suggestion conveyed by a person of high reputation; but the same effect can be often achieved also by the use of commanding tones in trance induction.

"Repeated prestige suggestion produces no more marked effect than does a single suggestion in changing social attitudes. However, the results seem to be more lasting with repeated suggestion" (S. Glasner, in the *Journal of Clinical and Experimental Hypnosis,* 1953).

PROJECTION, SENSORY: The reference of sensations arising in one's mind to an appropriate outside source. This takes place in everyday experience, for instance in vision and hearing, as well as in ordinary sleep or a hypnotic state.

PSEUDO-PARALYSIS: Functional loss of muscular power, resembling paralysis. This can be treated by suggestion or hypnosis.

PSORIASIS, see: *"Dermatosis."*

PSYCHASTHENIA: A loose variety of neurotic conditions including anxiety states, compulsions, obsessions, and phobias. All of them require psychiatric treatment which may or may not include hypnosis.

PSYCHEISM: A term synonymous with mesmerism or animal magnetism.

PSYCHIATRIST: A physician specializing in mental ailments, defects, and deviations.

PSYCHIATRY: The science of mental pathology, generally regarded as a branch of medicine.

PSYCHOANALYSIS: The system or school of psychiatry developed by Sigmund Freud (1856-1939) and his followers, which attributes neurotic or deviant behavior to repressed factors in human instinctive life, particularly in "the unconscious." To restore mental health, the proponents of psychoanalysis use an elaborate technique of treatment, including dream interpretation.

"Psychoanalytic treatment becomes a personal battlefield between the patient, who seeks to cling to his compulsive trends, and the analyst, who strives to remove them" (L. A. Wolberg, *Hypnoanalysis*).

PSYCHOANALYST: The person professionally qualified to use the psychoanalytic technique.

PSYCHOANALYTIC: Pertaining to psychoanalysis or partaking of its qualities.

PSYCHOBIOLOGY: Though the term had been occasionally used before, it has now become definitely associated with a doctrine related to psychoanalysis and developed by Adolf Meyer, an American psychiatrist (1866-1950), who emphasized the importance of normal adjustment to one's environment.

PSYCHOCATHARSIS: A variety of cathartic treatment developed by L. Frank, which is conducted in the state of light hypnosis.

PSYCHODRAMA: A psychiatric technique of group treatment developed by J. L. Moreno (1892-), which emphasizes the process of 'acting out' one's problems and grievances in an appropriate social milieu. It is usually "best organized in a therapeutic theatre, but it may be carried out wherever the patient lives, if his problem requires it" (*Das Stegreif Theater*).

PSYCHOGENESIS: Psychological origin.

PSYCHOGENIC: Arising in mental experience, normal or abnormal. A psychogenic disorder originates in individuals unable or unwilling to face personal or social difficulties. All this "comes to involve physiological changes as a result of such mental conditions" (G. Newbold, in the *Mental Hypnosis Handbook*).

PSYCHONEUROSIS, see: *"Neurosis."*

PSYCHOSOMATIC: Pertaining to bodily changes stimulated or depressed through mental influences.

PSYCHOSOMATICS: The science of mind-body interdependence.

PSYCHOTHERAPEUTIC: Pertaining to or promoting psychotherapy.

PSYCHOTHERAPY: The treatment of certain disorders, primarily mental, by various psychological methods ranging from persuasion, re-education, Christian Science, Alcoholics Anonymous, and psychoanalysis to suggestion and hypnosis.

"Psychotherapy derives its significance from the fact that the causative factor in the development of certain diseases is psychological in origin. That is why neuroses happen to form the most important area in the development and application of psychotherapy" (V. N. Miassischev, in the *Psychotherapy in the Soviet Union*).

PSYCHOTIC: Pertaining to or affected by one of the psychoses.

PULSE: The rhythmic wave of tension in the arteries, caused by heart action.

"The induction of hypnosis is sometimes accompanied by an acceleration of the pulse. This, although regarded as a characteristic phenomenon by some authorities, appears to be due to emotional causes alone; for, although it frequently appears the first time hypnosis is induced, it rarely occurs afterward" (J. M. Bramwell, *Hypnotism, Its History, Practice and Theory*).

PUYSÉGUR, ARMAND J. M. C., Marquis de: An outstanding follower of Mesmer and author of *Du Magnétisme Animal* (1807), who introduced certain modifications into the theory and practice of hypnosis. Having found suggestion of convulsions undesirable, he developed instead a sleep-like state called by him "artificial somnambulism," or trance (1784). He also noticed occasional occurrence of spontaneous amnesia, and realized that whatever cures could be achieved by means of hypnosis must be related to personal beliefs and their connection with the human organism.

R

RAPPORT: Working relationship between the hypnotist and his subject; adequate susceptibility of the latter to suggestions voiced by the former. Rapport can be deliberately transferred to another person and, at a pre-arranged signal, back again to the hypnotist. But, unless it is transferred by a special suggestion, rapport is exclusive. The subject, once hypnotized, listens only to the operator.

"Others present may talk to him, shout orders and give suggestions, but he ignores them as completely as if they were on the planet Mars" (G. H. Estabrooks, *Hypnotism*).

"A person who falls asleep spontaneously is in rapport with himself, while a hypnotized subject is in rapport with the person who hypnotized him" (A. Moll, *The Study of Hypnosis*).

"The phenomenon called rapport is never encountered unless suggested to the subject either directly or indirectly" (C. L. Hull, *Hypnosis and Suggestibility*).

RATIONALIZATION: Wishful thinking; convenient justification of an act; specious explanation.

RECORDING, PHONOGRAPH OR TAPE: Mechanical devices in the service of hypnotic practice. Among the pioneers in this field is G. H. Estabrooks who reported on his work in the *American Journal of Psychology*, 1930. It is advisable, for an experienced operator to be always present during any such session, simply because "no record, no matter how skillfully devised, can meet the various emergencies which arise when we induce the trance" (G. H. Estabrooks, *Hypnotism*).

REGRESSION, AGE, see: *"Age Regression."*

RELAXATION: Persons who are inclined to be emotional and consequently tense can be trained to relax by means of hypnosis. Dr. S. J. Van Pelt reports, for instance, the case of a middle-aged man with the blood pressure of 240 who was successfully taught, under light hypnosis, how to relax; more specifically, he learned to "deal with his problems without developing nervous tension."

RELAXATION, PROGRESSIVE: Training how to relax increasingly by being subjected to repeated suggestions in a series of hypnotic sessions.

RESISTANCE: Some subjects are unwilling to be hypnotized, for reasons of their own, even after they have given consent to that effect. Or else they manifest resistance to some particular suggestion if, for instance, it happens to be contrary to their convictions or moral beliefs. In extreme cases, they may even break the hypnotic state. This phenomenon is regarded by some experts as justifiable protection of subjects against careless or unscrupulous amateur-hypnotists. It may also serve as an occasional lesson to be more tactful and considerate of the subject's feelings.

"The power that we acquire over those individuals who are brought in the hypnotic condition is complete only when it concerns their health and welfare. Apart from this they can be made to perform various harmless actions, such as moving about, dancing or singing; in short, whatever anybody else might do under ordinary circumstances. But there are limits beyond which this power does not extend; and we can say quite definitely that every experienced hypnotist knows full well that whenever his suggestions become unacceptable to the subject with regard to his convictions and moral character, he is almost certain to manifest strong resistance" (A. Puységur, *Du Magnétisme Animal*).

RETROACTIVE INHIBITION: The tendency of all new experience, except understanding, to weaken and undermine previously learned material in the same field. But this process can be reversed by appropriate hypnotic suggestions so as to revive faint and apparently lost memories. See: "*Hypermnesia.*"

RIGIDITY, HYPNOTIC: A state of muscular contraction occasionally arising in deep hypnosis.

"One of the best known features in hypnosis is the rigidity of the whole body. There is sometimes a complete tonic contracture of nearly all the voluntary muscles, through which the head, neck, trunk, and legs become as stiff as a board. A well-known experiment can be carried out in this state: the head can be placed on one chair and the feet on another, and the body will not double up. A heavy weight, that of a man, for example, may even be placed upon the body without bending it. It is not astonishing, after what I have said of the effect of the mesmeric passes, that this stiffening should be more easily induced by their means; it cannot always be induced by mere verbal suggestions. A command or sign of the experimenter generally suffices to put an end to the rigidity" (A. Moll, *Hypnotism*).

RULES OF SAFETY: Professional ethics in any branch of medicine or psychology includes rules for the protection of all concerned. In the practice of hypnosis such rules have been suggested by H. M. Bernheim in his *Suggestive Therapeutics,* namely:

1. "Never hypnotize any subject without his formal consent, or the consent of those in authority over him."

2. "Never induce hypnotic sleep except in the presence of a third person in authority, who can guarantee the good faith of the hypnotist as well as the subject. Thus any trouble may be avoided in the event of an accusation."

3. "Never give to the hypnotized subject any other suggestions than those required for his cure."

S

SALPETRIÈRE SCHOOL: The neurological clinic in Paris organized by J. M. Charcot (1878). It was conducted on the controversial assumption that the phenomena of hypnosis are related to hysteria.

SCHILDER, PAUL F. (1886-1940): An American hypnotist and advocate of group therapy.
"The fact that one member of the group brings forward material which another very often tries to hide lessens the resistance. . . . It is easier to see one's own problem when it is brought forward by another" (*Psychotherapy*).

SCIENTIFIC APPROACH: "I think it indispensable that science should take possession of hypnotism. This is the easiest way to prevent its misuse. When I speak of science I naturally mean psychology as well as medicine, for hypnotism will never become a factor in medicine without a scientific psychological basis. Psychology is needed for the investigation of mental states just as chemistry and physics are needed for the testing of drugs and the investigation of electricity. But just as medicine is obliged in part to leave the study of chemical and physical agents to the representatives of other sciences, so it will be obliged not only to leave the investigation of hypnotism to psychologists, but to beg them to undertake it" (A. Moll, *Hypnotism*).

SÉANCE: Performance of hypnosis in the presence of a group of observers.

SELECTIVE AMNESIA: Amnesia confined to a specific area of experience.

SELF-HYPNOSIS, see: *"Auto-hypnosis."*

SELF-SUGGESTION, see: *"Auto-suggestion."*

SIGNAL, IDEOMOTOR: Such a signal made by a subject in a hypnotic state usually assumes the form of small, repetitive movements, such as finger jerks. These movements serve as signs of protest or distress; if disregarded, they are likely only to increase in vigor.

"When there are contradictions between verbal and ideomotor answers, the ideomotor one has proven more reliable on the basis of subsequent checking" (D. B. Cheek, in the *American Journal of Clinical Hypnosis*, V. 2).

96

SLEEP: A natural and usually quiet state of bodily and mental relaxation, in which consciousness may be suspended or assume the form of dreams.

"Sleep induced by hypnosis," contends Dr. A. P. Magonet referring specifically to cases of insomnia, "has advantages which far outweigh those of drug-induced sleep" (*Hypnosis in Medicine*).

"Hypnotic sleep is one of the most valuable forms of remedial protective inhibition" (B. V. Andreyev, *Sleep Therapy in the Neuroses*).

"It is possible to transform sleep into hypnosis or hypnosis into sleep. . . . In the latter case the rapport at once ceases" (G. W. Jacoby, *Suggestion and Psychotherapy*).

SLEEP, HYPNOTIC: The state of hypnosis.

"Of all the circumstances connected with Hypnotic Sleep, nothing so strongly marks the difference between it and natural sleep as the wonderful power the former evinces in curing many diseases of long standing, and which had resisted natural sleep and every known agency for years" (James Braid, *Neurypnology*).

"Let us make it perfectly clear *what* we are suggesting when we hypnotize. If we say to the patient, 'Sleep!' why does he not pass into ordinary slumber? Unless we agree that hypnosis is the same thing as normal sleep (and we have already refuted this hypothesis), the formula of 'suggested sleep' is insufficient to account for the phenomena. If we wish to maintain that hypnosis is due to suggestion, we have to admit that the very fact of putting anyone to sleep by suggestion gives the sleep a peculiar character. The question then arises, *By what mechanism does this peculiar character originate?* (Edouard Claparède, in the *Journal fuer Psychologie und Neurologie*).

97

"The command to sleep in hypnosis means nothing more or less than an order to withdraw all interest from the world and to concentrate it upon the person of the hypnotist. And it is so understood by the subject; for in this withdrawal of interest from the outer world lies the psychological characteristic of sleep, and the kinship between sleep and the state of hypnosis is based upon it" (Sigmund Freud, *Group Psychology and the Analysis of the Ego*).

"Reflexes are usually the same during hypnosis as in the normal waking state, but are considerably lessened during (ordinary) sleep" (S. Edmunds, *Hypnotism and the Supernormal*).

"The hypnotized subject seldom remembers, on awakening, the events which occurred during his hypnotic sleep" (A. Binet and C. Féré, *Animal Magnetism*).

SLEEP WALKING, see: *"Somnambulism."*

SMOKING: "Smoking is an easily acquired addiction and, consequently, it is usually associated with all kinds of phenomena of everyday life. My own experience with a large number of cured smokers seems to indicate that a more conscientious and careful selection of the therapeutic measures is indicated in each case. . . .

"It is necessary to distinguish among several stages of the kind of treatment we propose. The first stage consists in the examination of the smoker's personality, the compelling reasons for turning to smoking as well as for wishing to quit smoking. The second stage amounts to the registration of all the relevant and significant facts, sensations and experiences during smoking or during abstention from smoking. The third stage, following an exhaustive study of the individual, is devoted to treatment under hypnosis. . . .

"Hypnotic suggestion itself, which culminates the progress of treatment, is not necessarily the most important part of it. We turn to it only when the patient has been thoroughly prepared for it. Putting the patient into the hypnotic state aims only at creating the most favorable conditions for consolidating the results of treatment. And the state of hypnosis is undoubtedly the best state in which to receive suggestion. . . .

"In most instances, cessation of smoking takes place after the first session. But it is always desirable to have another session the following day and again two days later" (Y. A. Povorinsky, in the *Psychotherapy in the Soviet Union*).

SODIUM PENTOTHAL: This drug (as also sodium amytal) has been used in small doses to increase the subject's suggestibility.

SOMNAMBULE: The person in the state of deep hypnosis.

"A somnambule is far from being, as some writers assert, an unconscious automaton, devoid of judgment, reason and intellectual spontaneity. On the contrary, his memory is excellent, his intelligence is active, and his imagination is highly excited" (A. Binet and C. Féré, *Animal Magnetism*).

SOMNAMBULISM: I. Sleep-walking. This is a condition in which the individual is walking in his dream and even performing fairly complex tasks while being for all practical purposes asleep. Like any normal sleeper, such a person will be subsequently unable to recall his behavior during the state.

"There are three stages generally distinguished in somnambulism.

"First. — That in which the sleeper speaks.

99

"Second. — That in which he makes all sorts of movements, but does not leave his chair or bed.

"Third. — That in which he gets up, walks about and performs the most complicated actions" (A. Moll, *Hypnotism*).

II. Deep hypnosis or trance.

"One out of every five subjects will, on the average, go into deep hypnosis or somnambulism" (G. H. Estabrooks, *Hypnotism*).

"In this state the eyes may be opened without waking, complete amnesia is usual, positive and negative hallucinations may be induced" (S. J. Van Pelt, in the *Medical Hypnosis Handbook*).

"There are somnambulists who sleep with open eyes; and my experience has proved that these are somnambulists by nature" (Abbé Faria, *De la cause du sommeil lucide*).

SOMNAMBULISM, ARTIFICIAL: A. Puységur's term for the hypnotic trance.

SOMNAMBULISM, MONOIDEIC: A form of sleep walking in which the person's actions are consistently repetitious.

SOMNAMBULISM, POLYIDEIC: A form of sleep walking in which the person's actions vary each time.

SPEECH THERAPY: Insofar as practically all communication between human beings involves speech, it is inevitable that some of it will be used for medical or psychological purposes, directly or indirectly. Psychoanalysis uses it directly and purposefully; the confessional technique of various churches uses it indirectly, by relieving one's conscience. The therapeutic influence of talk covers a large field including: *persuasion*

100

well grounded in facts and reasons and assuming the form of explanation, clarification, assurance, and encouragement; direct or indirect *suggestion,* in individual or group relations; and *hypnosis.*

"Insofar as verbal stimulations act upon the cortex, speech therapy must be regarded as a basic treatment for all psychogenic disturbances, though used in a variety of ways. Consequently, it has several purposes, namely:

"(1) To determine the actual causes leading to, and calling forth, functional disturbances of the higher nervous system.

"(2) To remove the operation of the factors which functionally weaken the cortex, including various forms of negative emotions.

"(3) To overcome or reduce serious functional disturbances of the higher nervous activities, among them disruption of any normal dynamic stereotypy.

"(4) To create new and adequate cortical connections and thus to restore the patient's working ability.

"(5) To enable the patient to get adjusted to the conditions of his external environment, thus preventing the likelihood of recurring disturbances in the future" (K. I. Platonov, in the *Psychotherapy in the Soviet Union*).

STATUVOLENCE: Self-induced hypnosis.

STUPOROUS TRANCE: The state of deep hypnosis.

STUTTERING: In its earlier stages, stuttering (or stammering) manifests itself mainly in emotional situations and indicates an incipient neurosis. But chronic cases are complex and deep-rooted; they demand extensive specialized treatment, preferably involving social relations with cases of their own kind. The Hospital for Speech Disorders in New York City is doing considerable clinical work in this connection as well as some research. Hypnosis can be used with good effect in these cases. But, insofar as stuttering usually begins early, the best time for the treatment of any case is childhood.

"A psychotherapeutic activity which makes speech easier for the child consists in musical rhythmical exercises, known as logorhythmic and introduced by V. A. Guiliarovky. During these exercises speech is combined with music and motions. A child, in listening to music together with other children, does not pay much attention to speech and is thus enabled to utter words without self-consciousness" (N. A. Vlassova, in the *Psychotherapy in the Soviet Union*).

SUBCONSCIOUSNESS: The state in which mental processes and possibly the resulting behavior take place apart from one's conscious awareness.

SUBJECT: An individual used for psychological experimentation or hypnosis.
"The more intelligent, the more extraverted, and the stronger willed the person is, the more likely he is to be a good hypnotic subject" (M. H. Erickson, S. Hershman, and I. I. Secter, *The Practical Application of Medical and Dental Hypnosis*).

SUGGESTIBILITY: Susceptibility to suggestion. Excessive suggestibility indicates weakness of character; but a certain degree of it is perfectly normal. W. McDougall derives it from the animal instinct of submission; according to him "the human species also is endowed with this instinct of submission" (*Outline of Abnormal Psychology*).
"The popular belief that suggestibility is a mark of stupidity

102

or lack of intelligence appears to be wholly an error" (C. L. Hull, *Hypnosis and Suggestibility*).

"A large number of studies . . . failed to find reliable relationships between hypnotizability or suggestibility and traits of personality" (T. X. Barber, *Psychological Reports*, 1964).

SUGGESTIBILITY, NEGATIVE: Reaction to suggestion by doing the opposite.

SUGGESTION: A hint, proposal, offer of a new or alternative idea, given in the waking state or otherwise. In hypnosis, it is a technique of influencing a subject or of modifying his behavior.

"Whatever suggestion has done, suggestion can undo" (Charles Baudouin, *Suggestion and Autosuggestion*).

"Suggestion is more active in primitive people than it is in sophisticated Western peoples" (Ainslie Meares, "Atavistic Theory of Hypnosis," in the *Transactions of the* 1961 *International Congress on Hypnosis*).

"We can regard suggestion as the simplest form of conditioned reflex in man" (I. P. Pavlov, *Conditioned Reflexes*).

"People are not convinced by truth but by suggestion. The explanation of the success of Hitler or of dozens of other figures of history can be accounted for only on this basis" (V. F. Calverton, *The Man Inside*).

"Suggestion is one of the most influential forces in our life. . . . Many nervous weaknesses and faulty habits can be corrected in children by means of suggestion made during sleep. Children do not wake up easily when spoken to in sleep, hence suggestive therapeutics may be employed with them. To be most effective such suggestions should be made by the

103

mother or some other person who is on intimate friendly relations with the child. Childish fears, sleep-walking, enuresis, nervous twitchings, unpleasant dispositions, and similar nervous reactions and faulty habits have been known to respond to suggestions made during sleep. Suggestions operate during the waking state, in the state of complete relaxation and hypnosis, and in the sleep state. It depends on external stimuli for its operation" (A. D. Mueller, "Suggestion," in the *Encyclopedia of Child Guidance,* ed. by R. B. Winn).

"Suggestion plays a very important part in hypnotism. We can influence common sensation very materially by suggestion in hypnosis. This is not surprising when we consider that it is exactly the common sensations which are most under the influence of mental processes. Just as looking down from a tower causes giddiness, as the thought of repugnant food produces disgust, so we can call up these and related phenomena, or cause them to disappear. It is in this direction that suggestion has to record its most striking successes, since the common sensations, of which *pain* is one, are the cause of most of the complaints we hear. As pain, etc., can be induced by suggestion, so by suggestion it can often be banished. I say to a subject who complains of want of appetite, 'The loss of appetite has disappeared, you are hungry.' I can cause another to feel thirst. Feelings of pleasure can likewise be excited" (A. Moll, *Hypnotism*).

SUGGESTION, EMOTIONAL MECHANISM OF: The function of this mechanism is largely unconscious, insofar as it involves the autonomic nervous system. It can organize or disorganize human activity, which is clearly shown in the following imaginative passage:

"Lay upon the group a plank thirty feet long and nine

104

inches wide. Everyone will be able to walk along this plank without putting a foot to the ground on either side. Now change the conditions of the experiment. Let the plank connect the twin towers of a cathedral, and tell me who will be able to walk for a yard along this narrow pathway. Do you think you will be able to? You could not make a couple of steps without beginning to tremble; and then, despite all your efforts of will, you would inevitably fall" (E. Coué, *De la Suggestion et de ses Applications*).

"No matter how hard you may work for success, if your thought is saturated with the fear of failure, it will kill your efforts, neutralize your endeavors, and make success impossible" (O. S. Marden, *The Miracle of Right Thought*).

SUGGESTION, INDIRECT: Suggestion administered in a manner that finds the subject unprepared, unable to oppose it.

SUGGESTION, NEGATIVE: Suggestion not to do something. It is always preferable to re-word it in a positive way.

SUGGESTION, POST-HYPNOTIC: Suggestion given by a hypnotist to his subject, to be carried out subsequently in the waking state.

SUGGESTION, THERAPEUTIC: Suggestion aiming at the restoration of somebody's health or serving some purpose of medical treatment.

SUGGESTION, VERBAL, see: *"Verbal Suggestion."*

SUGGESTION, WAKING: "Any theory of suggestion must take into account waking suggestion equally with hypnotic suggestion" (W. McDougall, *Outline of Abnormal Psychology*).

SUGGEST, TO: To offer a new or alternative choice in the form of action, experience, attitude, or idea.

SYNGIGNOCISM: The same as hypnotism (rare).

T

TAPE RECORDER, see: *"Recording, Phonograph or Tape."*

TENSION: The experience of strain or attentive waiting. "The fear gives rise to tension . . . the tension, especially if not dispersed in action, upsets the balance of the autonomic nervous system which in turn gives rise to unpleasant symptoms" (S. J. Van Pelt, in the *Medical Hypnosis Handbook*).

TESTS OF HYPNOTIC READINESS, see: *"Eyeball Set Test," "Hand Clasping Test,"* and *"Postural Sway Test."*

THEORIES OF HYPNOSIS: The history of scientific hypnotism offers a considerable number of theories ranging

107

from sheer speculation to hypotheses grounded in solid facts. But each of them offers no more than partial explanation of the phenomena. The final synthesis is yet to be achieved.

The modern use of hypnosis begins with F. A. Mesmer (1734-1815) who contended that the treatment of hysteria and other human ailments by means of hypnosis worked because it redistributed the forces of "animal magnetism," to be distinguished from the familiar "mineral" magnetism. More specifically, he claimed that these magnetic forces originating among the stars could be controlled by passes he used and thus influence the circulation of fluids within the patient's body. On his arrival to Paris, Mesmer elaborated his technique to change it into group treatment. The success of his work attracted a great deal of public attention, until the French Academy appointed an investigating committee (1784), which discounted Mesmer's claims.

See: *"Baquet," "Mesmer,"* and *"Mesmerism."*

James Braid (1795-1860), a Manchester physician, realized that magnetism of any kind had nothing to do with the phenomena of hypnotism. The force behind it, he contended, was suggestion on the part of the operator and concentrated attention on the part of the subject, which resulted in a state resembling sleep and could indeed be used successfully in medical treatments and surgery. The latter application of hypnosis was soon demonstrated by his contemporary, James Esdaile (1808-1859), practicing in India.

See: *"Braid," "Braidism," "Esdaile,"* and *"Monoideism."*

But the phenomenon of suggestion itself needed an explanation. To meet this problem, J. M. Charcot (1825-1893) of the Salpêtrière hospital in Paris assumed that the hypnotic trance was merely a state of artificial hysteria and that, consequently, it represented the phenomenon of a divided mind.

Among the scholars influenced by this view were Pierre Janet (1859-1947), with his theory of dissociation of personality, and Morton Prince (1854-1929).

See: *"Charcot"* and *"Dissociation."*

An entirely different approach to the problem was taken by I. P. Pavlov (1849-1936), according to whom sleep and hypnosis are related ony in the sense that both are but different manifestations of inhibitory processes. More specifically, "hypnosis is inhibition spread over the usually active points in special areas of the hemispheres" (*Scientific Monthly,* 1923). Nevertheless, he did acknowledge that phenomena of hypnosis may manifest also effects of facilitation. In short, then, Pavlov as well as V. M. Bekhterev (1857-1927) were of the opinion that hypnosis was fundamentally a neural phenomenon controlled by the autonomic nervous system and the processes of conditioning.

See: *"Autonomic Nervous System," "Bekhterev, V. M.," "Conditioned Reflex," "Facilitation," "Inhibition,"* and *"Pavlov, I. P."*

More recently, a number of scholars have come to endorse the view that hypnosis is a kind of regression to the past. According to S. Ferenczi, a Hungarian psychoanalyst, the hypnotic state represents regression to infancy, whereas J. M. Schneck takes it to be regression to a primitive level, while A. Meares upholds essentially the same view, but calls it an "atavistic" theory of hypnosis.

See: *"Regression."*

There is one fact, however, on which all the contemporary authorities may agree, and it is, to quote C. Hull, that "the only thing which seems to characterize hypnosis as such and which gives any justification for the practice of calling it a 'state' is its generalized hypersuggestibility. The difference between the hypnotic state and the normal one is, therefore, a quantitative rather than a qualitative one" (*Hypnosis and Suggestibility*).

See: *"Hypersuggestibility."*

THERAPEUTICS, SUGGESTIVE: The use of hypnosis or suggestion for medical or psychological treatment.

"I begin by saying to the patient that I believe benefit is to be derived from the use of suggestive therapeutics, that it is possible to cure or at least to relieve him by hypnotism; that there is nothing either hurtful or strange about it; that it is an ordinary sleep or torpor which can be induced in everyone, and that this quiet, beneficial condition restores the equilibrium of the nervous system. If necessary, I hypnotize one or two subjects in his presence, in order to show him that there is nothing painful in this condition, and that it is not accompanied with any unusual sensation. When I have thus banished from his mind the idea of magnetism and the somewhat mysterious fear that attaches to that unknown condition, above all when he has seen patients cured or benefited by the means in question he is no longer suspicious, but gives himself up, then I say, '*Look at me, and think of nothing but sleep;* your eyelids begin to feel heavy; your eyes are tired; they begin to wink; they are getting moist; you cannot see distinctly; they are closed.' Some patients close their eyes and are asleep immediately. With others, I have to repeat again and yet again, and lay more stress on what I say, and even make gestures" (H. M. Bernheim, *Suggestive Therapeutics*).

THUMB-SUCKING: A common habit of small children which must be regarded, when extended beyond the age of four years, as a neurotic symptom. The habit can be readily relieved by hypnosis, but may require also psychiatric treatment for complete restoration of mental health.

TIC: Spasmodic twitching of a muscle, usually of nervous origin.

TIME DISTORTION: Acceleration or slowing down of the human sense of time — as during a gay party or waiting in a dentist's office, respectively. This phenomenon can be readily demonstrated also by means of hypnotic suggestion.

TIME SENSE: Normal awareness of the passage of time.

"The experiences of an individual appear to us arranged in a series of events; in this series the single events which we remember appear to be ordered according to the criterion of 'earlier' and 'later.' There exists, therefore, for the individual, an I-time, or subjective time. This in itself is not measurable" (Albert Einstein, *The Meaning of Relativity*).

"Time sense can be controlled, within limits, hypnotically" (Henry Guze, in the *Annual Review of Hypnosis Literature*, 1953).

"Time sense can be deliberately altered by hypnotic suggestion. Thus a ten-second interval by the clock might seem to be one or ten minutes to the hypnotized subject. Furthermore, the individual concerned might report that he had had an amount of subjective experience in the form of hallucinated activities, thought, feeling, and the like — all proceeding at a normal rate — that was more nearly appropriate to the subjective ten minutes than to the brief ten seconds recorded by the clock. One of the inferences from these results is that mental activity, under the conditions described, can take

111

place at extremely rapid rates while appearing, to the subject, to progress at customary speeds" (L. F. Cooper and M. H. Erickson).

TRANCE: The state of hypnotic awareness. It is now customary to distinguish among several forms of it: light, medium, deep, and stuporous. These forms should be used according to the requirements of hypnotic treatment or experimentation.

TRANCE-COMA: The deep sleep following a hypnotic session.

TRANCE INDUCTION: The process or technique of hypnotizing the subject. The basic principles of this can be described under three headings: (a) Concentration of the subject's attention on something, say, on a suspended metallic ball, small revolving mirror, or the process of counting. No choice of objects of observation should be allowed. (b) Dividing the subject's attention, usually between the hypnotist's voice and the object of observation. And (c) Emphasis on relaxation and increasing drowsiness.

All such methods can be arranged, however, in many different ways. For instance, Mesmer created in his studio a highly elaborate system of strange objects and used "passes." Liébeault was in the habit of bringing the fingers of his right hand closer and closer to the subject's face and finally saying "Sleep!" Braid employed the method of "fascination" by means of a bright object. Dr. Luys preferred revolving mirrors attached to bars arranged in a T-form. Charcot devised the technique of challenge beginning with the words "You can't. . . ."

112

If the subject appears to be difficult to start with, he may be allowed to watch an advanced subject falling into the trance, before he himself is hypnotized.

Evening sessions (after school, work, etc.) are on the whole preferable, mainly because the subject is likely to be relaxed.

TRANSFER: Suggested transfer of a subject's rapport from the hypnotist himself to another person, for instance, an assistant or a lecturer. But the subject must be informed in advance that, at a certain signal, the original rapport will be restored.

TRAUMATIC EXPERIENCE: An emotional shock and its possible effect on the person's health, personality, and emotions.

U

UNCONDITIONED REFLEX: An original or innate reflex as opposed to a learned or conditioned reflex.

UNCONSCIOUSNESS: Lack or loss of consciousness. "Mental processes are largely unconscious" (S. Freud, *A General Introduction to Psychoanalysis*). "Unconscious ideas . . . include conscious states that we are not aware of" (Morton Prince, *The Unconscious*).

UNDERSTANDING: The mental function of making experience meaningful and realistically usable. It is an organizational factor bringing order into the complexity of human observations, feelings and actions. Its effectiveness is highly correlated with good memory.

U

V

VERBAL SUGGESTION: Suggestion by means of words carefully chosen.

"Verbal stimuli serve as effective instigation of hypnotic dreams" (D. B. Klein, in the *University of Texas Bulletin* No. 3009, 1930).

See also: *"Ideoplasty."*

VICTROLA RECORDS, see: *"Recording, Phonograph or Tape."*

W

WAKING: Return from the hypnotic state to the familiar state of waking consciousness. This does not always take place momentarily, and the subject should not be hurried.

WAKING HYPNOSIS: A state of waking in which the subject is actually under the influence of a post-hypnotic suggestion.

WAKING SUGGESTION, see: *"Suggestion, Waking."*

WISHFUL THINKING: "It is the general experience that the human intellect errs very easily without our suspecting it at all, and that nothing is more readily believed than what

119

— regardless of the truth — meets our wishes and illusions halfway" (S. Freud, *Moses and Monotheism*).

"Wishful thinking, by virtue of which one is usually right while the opponent is usually wrong, is an everyday phenomenon and no one is entirely free from it. It molds one's reaction to events, it permeates one's political activities, it determines one's choice of books and entertainment, it decides the questions of love and hatred" (*Scientific Hypnotism*).

See also: *"Rationalization."*

WORDS: "Words can serve as real conditioning stimuli beyond any quantitative or qualitative comparison with any other stimulation in life" (I. P. Pavlov, *Clinical Environments*).

"There is not an organ or tissue in the human body the condition of which cannot be modified in one manner or another by means of words, that is to say, by way of the cortex" (K. I. Platonov, in the *Psychotherapy in the Soviet Union*).

WORK THERAPY: Treatment by means of fruitful and satisfying occupation.

See: *"Occupational Therapy."*

Z

ZOIST, THE: The journal organized by Dr. John Elliotson (1791-1868) and devoted to the discussion of new medical problems, in which Dr. James Esdaile (1808-1859) published his accounts of surgical operations performed under hypnosis in India.

ZOOMAGNETISM, see: *"Animal Magnetism."*

SELECTED BIBLIOGRAPHY

Ambrose, G., and Newbold, G., *A Handbook of Medical Hypnosis.* Williams and Wilkins Co., 1958.

American Journal of Clinical Hypnosis (since 1958). Editor: M. H. Erickson. 32 W. Cypress St., Phoenix, Arizona.

Andreyev, B. V., *Sleep Therapy in the Neuroses.* Consultants' Bureau, 1960.

Annual Review of Hypnosis Literature (since 1953), a Publication of the Society for Clinical and Experimental Hypnosis. The Woodrow Press, Inc., 227 E. 45 St., New York 17, N. Y.

Barber, T. X., "Hypnotizability, Suggestibility, and Personality," *Psychological Reports,* 1964.

Baudouin, Charles, *Suggestion and Autosuggestion.* Dodd, Mead and Co.

Bekhterev, V. M., *General Principles of Human Reflexology.* International Publishers.

Bernheim, H. M., *Suggestive Therapeutics.* Associated Booksellers, 1957.

Binet, A., and Féré, C., *Animal Magnetism.* D. Appleton and Co., 1888.

Braid, James, *Braid on Hypnotism.* Julian Press, 1960.

Bramwell, J. M., *Hypnotism, Its History and Theory.* Julian Press, 1959.

Brennan, M., and Gill, M., *Hypnotherapy.* International Universities Press, 1947.

British Journal of Medical Hypnotism. 48 Wick Hall, Hove 2, Sussex, England.

Charcot, J. M., *Lectures on the Diseases of the Nervous System.* The New Sydenham Society, 1889.

Cook, W. W., *Practical Lessons in Hypnotism.* Castle Books, 1901.

Cooper, L. F., and Erickson, M. H., *Time Distortion in Hypnosis.* Williams and Wilkins Co., 1959.

Coué, Emile, *How to Practice Suggestion and Autosuggestion.* American Library Service, 1923.

Coué, Emile, *Self-Mastery through Conscious Autosuggestion.* American Library Service, 1922.

Cuddon, Eric, *Hypnosis, Its Meaning and Practice.* Bell, London, 1955.

Dorcus, K. M., *Hypnosis and Its Therapeutic Applications*. McGraw Hill, 1956.

Edmunds, Simeon, *Hypnotism and the Supernormal*. Aquarian Press, 1961.

Erickson, M. H., Hershman, S., and Secter, I. I., *The Practical Applications of Medical and Dental Hypnosis*. Julian Press, 1961.

Esdaile, M. H., *Hypnosis in Medicine and Surgery*. Julian Press, 1957.

Estabrooks, G. H., *Hypnosis, Current Problems*. Harper & Row, 1962.

Estabrooks, G. H., *Hypnotism*. E. P. Dutton, 1957.

Eysenck, H. J., "Suggestibility and Hypnosis — an Experimental Analysis," *Proceedings of the Royal Soc. of Medicine*, 1943.

Faria, Abbé, *De la cause du sommeil lucide*. Reprinted, H. Jouve, Paris, 1906.

Forel, August, *Hypnotism and Psychotherapy*. Rebman Co., 1907.

Goldsmith, M., *Franz Anton Mesmer*. Doubleday, Doran & Co., 1934.

Grinker, R. R., and Spiegel, J. P., *War Neuroses*. Blakiston Co., 1945.

Hammerschlag, H. E., *Hypnotism and Crime*. Rider, London, 1956.

Hull, C. L., *Hypnosis and Suggestibility*. D. Appleton-Century, (1933).

Jacoby, G. W., *Suggestion and Psychotherapy*. Ch. Scribner's, 1912.

Janet, Pierre, *Psychological Healing*. Macmillan Co., 1925.

Jenness, Arthur, "Hypnotism," in *Personality and Behavior Disorders*, I. Ed. by J. McV. Hunt, Ronald Press, 1944.

Journal of Clinical and Experimental Hypnosis (since 1953). Woodrow Press, Inc., 227 E. 45 St., New York 17, N. Y.

Kline, M. V. (ed.), *Hypnodynamic Psychology*. Julian Press, 1955.

Kline, M. V. (ed.), *The Nature of Hypnosis*. Institute for Research in Hypnosis and the Postgraduate Center for Psychotherapy, (1962).

Krebs, S. L., *The Fundamental Principles of Hypnosis*. Julian Press, 1957.

Le Cron, L. M. (ed.), *Experimental Hypnosis*. Macmillan Co., 1952.

Le Cron, L. M., *Techniques of Hypnotherapy*. Julian Press, 1961.

Le Cron, L. M., and Bordeaux, J., *Hypnotism Today*, Grune & Stratton, 1947.

Liébeault, A. A., *Du sommeil et des états analogues*. V. Masson et fils, Paris, 1886.

Lindner, R. M., *Rebel without a Cause;* the Hypnoanalysis of a Criminal Psychopath. Grune & Stratton, 1944.

Magonet, A. P., *Hypnosis in Medicine*. Wilshire Book Co.

Marcuse, F. L., *Hypnosis: Fact and Fiction*. Penguin Books, 1959.

Marks, R. W., *The Story of Hypnotism*. Prentice-Hall, 1947.

Meares, A., *A System of Medical Hypnosis*. W. B. Saunders, 1960.

Moll, Albert, *Hypnotism*. Ch. Scribner's, 1913.

Moodie, William, *Hypnosis in Treatment*. Emerson Books, (1959).

123

Pavlov, I. P., "Inhibition, Hypnosis and Sleep," *Scientific Monthly*, 1923.

Powers, Melvin, *The Science of Hypnotism* (revised edition). Ottenheimer, Publ., 1953.

Rhodes, R. H., *Hypnosis: Theory, Practice and Application*. The Citadel Press, (1950).

Rhodes, R. H., *Therapy through Hypnosis*. The Citadel Press, (1961).

Rosen, H., *Hypnotherapy in Clinical Psychiatry*. Julian Press, 1953.

Rosenthal, R., and Wolfe, B., *Hypnotism Comes of Age*. Bobbs-Merrill, 1948.

Salter, Andrew, *What Is Hypnosis*. R. R. Smith, 1944.

Schilder, Paul, *The Nature of Hypnosis*. International Universities Press, 1956.

Schilder, P., and Kauders, O., "Hypnosis." *Nervous and Mental Disease Monograph Series*, No. 46, 1927.

Schneck, J. M., (ed.), *Hypnosis in Modern Medicine*. Blackwell Scientific Publ., Oxford, 1953.

Sidis, Boris, *The Psychology of Suggestion*. D. Appleton Co., 1921.

Stolzenberg, Jacob, *Psychosomatics and Suggestion Therapy in Dentistry*. Philosophical Library, (1950).

Van Pelt, S. J., *Hypnotic Suggestion*. Wright, Bristol, n. d.

Van Pelt, S. J., Ambrose, G., and Newbold, G., *Medical Hypnosis Handbook*. Wilshire Book Co., (1957).

Watkins, J. G., *Hypnotherapy of War Neuroses*. Ronald Press, 1949.

Weitzenhoffer, A. M., *Hypnotism*. J. Wiley & Sons, 1953.

Weitzenhoffer, A. M., *General Techniques of Hypnotism*. Grune & Stratton, 1957.

Wingfield, H. E., *An Introduction to the Study of Hypnotism*. Ballière Tindall, and Cox, 1920.

Winn, R. B., *Scientific Hypnotism*. Wilshire Book Co., (1956).

Winn, R. B. (ed.), *Psychotherapy in the Soviet Union*. Philosophical Library, (1961).

Wolberg, L. R., *Hypnoanalysis*. Grune & Stratton, 1945.

Wolberg, L. R., *Medical Hypnosis*. 2 vols. Grune & Stratton, 1948.